All one in Christ Jesus

'This is a book that needed writing. David Coffey asks some deep and searching questions which strike at the heart of why evangelicals are disunited. And, with passion, he urges us to work together prayerfully and honestly to seek some answers and some ways forward. Now the point is to do it.'

Pete Broadbent, Bishop of Willesden and
Chair of Spring Harvest/ICC

'This is a timely book. Evangelical unity is not a luxury, but is crucial to the vitality and credibility of our life and witness. David Coffey explores the theme with wisdom and conviction. He combines a firm grasp of Scripture with insights that reflect his pastoral heart and extensive experience as a church leader. Throughout my Christian life I've recognized the vast contribution that Keswick has made to evangelical unity and I pray that this helpful and accessible book will stimulate a deepening commitment to Christ-centred unity.'

The Revd Jonathan Edwards, General Secretary, Baptist
Union of Great Britain

'David's passion for unity and his challenge for others to step forward, to share the task of mending some of the broken bridges across the evangelical community, make this an important contribution to those facing the pain of divisions and reminds us of some of the biblical principles which need to be exercised as we explore our togetherness in Christ.'

Steve Clifford, Evangelical Alliance

'David Coffey writes with warmth and passion, inviting us to a renewal of gracious conversation in this most timely and practical book.'

Jeff Lucas, Author, Speaker, Broadcaster

'Realistic, practical, thoroughly biblical, and grounded in everyday life, this book is a deep cry from the heart of a man who knows what he's talking about. Echoing the strong NT call to unity, this book will both challenge and enrich its readers. We cannot afford to ignore what it says if we genuinely want to reach a watching world.'

Fran Beckett OBE – Leader of Restore (Peckham) and self-employed charity consultant

'In this powerful, timely and insightful book, David Coffey addresses a vital issue with clarity, honesty and courage. Coming from the pen of a Christian statesman who has "earned the right to be heard", this publication could transform the ecclesiastical landscape were its message to be welcomed and embraced.'

John Glass, General Superintendent, Elim Pentecostal Churches

'This is a valuable book on a crucial subject for today's evangelical community. David Coffey's heartfelt appeal to resist splintering and renew our commitment to evangelical unity is one we need to take to our hearts.'

John Risbridger, Above Bar church

'When as godly and gifted a peace-maker as David Coffey writes a passionate plea for greater evangelical unity, we had all better listen. Linking unity with effective evangelism, David tackles the issue of evangelical tribalism with disarming clarity and honesty. This urgent call for consensus on the essentials of biblical faith and unity in witness should be on every Christian leader's must-read list.'

Marcus Honeysett, Living Leadership Director

All one in Christ Jesus

David Coffey

MILTON KEYNES • COLORADO SPRINGS
• HYDERABAD

15 14 13 12 11 10 09   7 6 5 4 3 2 1

First published 2009 by Keswick Ministries and Authentic Media
9 Holdom Avenue, Bletchley, Milton Keynes, Bucks,
MK1 1QR, UK
1820 Jet Stream Drive, Colorado Springs, USA
OM Authentic Media, Jeedimetla Village
Secunderabad 500 055, A.P., India
www.authenticmedia.co.uk

Authentic Media is a division of IBS-STL U.K., limited by guarantee, with its
Registered Office at Kingstown Broadway, Carlisle, Cumbria CA3 0HA.
Registered in England & Wales No. 1216232. Registered charity 270162

British Library Cataloguing in Publication Data
A catalogue record for this book is available from the British
Library
ISBN-13: 978-1-85078-830-0

Cover design David Smart
Print Management by Adare
Printed in Great Britain by J.F. Print, Sparkford

Contents

Series Preface   ix
Introduction   xi

Part One – United we stand   1
1. All one in Christ Jesus   3
2. Why evangelical unity matters   9
3. Evangelicals fragmented   16

Part Two – The essentials of unity   25
4. Bind us together   27
5. Primary and secondary truth   38

Part Three – Issues that divide   47
6. Battles over the Bible   49
7. But the Bible says . . .   60

Part Four – Dangers to avoid   75
8. Insights from a housegroup   77
9. Disagreeing without being disagreeable   84

Part Five – Bridges to build   103
10. Bridges of reconciliation   105
11. Bridges of community   116
12. Bridges of witness   134

Epilogue – The world at one   143

   Acknowledgements   147
   Endnotes   150

Series Preface

For over 130 years, the Keswick Convention has played a vital role in the growth of the worldwide evangelical faith. However, there are millions of Christians who honour the name of Keswick but have limited appreciation of the Convention's core values and commitments. This exciting new series, *Keswick Foundations*, attempts to address that gap in understanding.

By providing key studies into some of the major emphases of the Convention, the prayer of its Trustees is that a new generation will be inspired afresh, in the words of its motto, to be 'All one in Christ Jesus'. Following the publication of the first title, *Discipleship* by Peter Maiden, this second volume in the series turns to the vital topic of evangelical unity. What are the primary gospel truths on which we stand? How do we handle legitimate diversity under the Lordship of Jesus? What is the unity of the Spirit? How are we to express our oneness in Christ in spite our different emphases?

Our respected author, David Coffey, President of the Baptist World Alliance, is no stranger to the kind of pressures such questions raise. Drawing on his extensive pastoral experience and his many contacts with the

church worldwide, he approaches the issues surrounding evangelical unity with grace, humility and not a
little humour. May this book help us all to 'go and do
likewise' (Lk. 10:37).

Welcome to a key 'Keswick Foundation'.

Steve Brady
Series Editor

Introduction

This is a book about evangelical unity. The founding vision of the Keswick movement began with the biblical conviction that those who confess Jesus is Lord, whatever their denominational affiliation, are 'All one in Christ Jesus.' The book does not deal with the issue of structured ecumenical unity between denominations, but it does focus on the need for a greater visible expression of unity between evangelicals.

Many of the biblical principles in this book will be rightly claimed by those who would not define themselves as evangelicals. I am not addressing the way we relate to the wider Christian church, although I do believe this is an important area for consideration, and can claim an extensive personal experience in relating as an evangelical to many of the world communions of the church. This book is a humble call to the evangelical family to take their own disunity more seriously and to put their own house in order.

Some of the chapters address issues of unity in the local church. It is in the local fellowship of believers that we learn the first principles of how our unity in Christ is expressed in diversity. In the local church, we learn how to handle diversity and then apply these principles in our wider fellowship with other Christians.

There are signs in all parts of the country of fruitful partnerships between evangelicals of different theological traditions. The numerous initiatives, local, national and international are not only a great encouragement but a clear sign it is possible to work within a reconciled diversity. These initiatives demonstrate that though we are not identical in every aspect of evangelical faith and practice, there is always sufficient ground for evangelical cooperation.

For all these encouragements, the current disunity among some of the tribes of evangelicalism is of critical importance. The divides and disagreements are serious in nature and need to be addressed. There are those who belong to the evangelical family by heritage who are ashamed of the name evangelical. There are those who claim to speak for all of us but whose graceless spirit and hectoring tone are a stain on the family name. There are broken relationships between leaders and organisations which remain unreconciled, to which we have all turned a blind eye. In recent years, new streams of evangelical life have emerged whose membership is drawn from many parts of the world, predominantly Africa, Latin America and South East Asia. These streams have brought with them a spiritual vitality and a dynamic understanding of evangelical faith which does not always fit comfortably with the more traditional expressions of evangelicalism. Have they been warmly welcomed and fully integrated into the breadth of life within British evangelicalism?

The burden of this book is that we are not meeting together in the way we should; we are not talking to each other in the way we should; we are not addressing the things that divide us; we are not seeking with urgency the fresh consensus on the essentials of evangelical faith which could contribute to a deeper expression of our unity; above all we are not one in mind in the single area where evangelicals have traditionally excelled – we are not united in God's mission. This book is written in the conviction that a greater unity can be achieved between the tribes.

- Part One addresses the meaning behind the verse 'All one in Christ Jesus' and considers some current examples of evangelical fragmentation and why evangelical unity matters.
- Part Two looks at the essentials of unity and explores some key biblical principles on which the church is founded. It explores the differences between primary and secondary truth.
- Part Three examines the issues which divide us, with particular emphasis on the authority of Scripture and some ground rules for interpreting the Bible.
- Part Four focuses on the local church and considers dangers to avoid in relating to other Christians, with some suggestions on how to disagree without being disagreeable. These principles have the widest application beyond the local fellowship.
- Part Five is about mending broken bridges, with illustrations on the healing of broken relationships; the strengthening of Christian community with special reference to accountability and church discipline; and the urgent need for a greater unity in mission and evangelism in a broken world.

I have written other books but I have never felt the burden of pain that I have had while writing this one. It is my prayer that others, who share this vision for the fullest expression of evangelical unity, will be courageous in stepping forward to share in the task of mending the broken bridges of the evangelical family.

David Coffey
Easter 2009

Part one

United we stand

Chapter One

All one in Christ Jesus

They had each seen the advert in a Christian magazine. It was for a Christian singles houseparty taking place over a long weekend in the New Year. On the first evening, nine of them sat round having a late night drink in the hotel lounge and informally introduced themselves to each other.

Alan worked for a Japanese car manufacturer based in Sunderland and spent his summer vacations leading youth groups on mountain climbing expeditions in Scotland. Brian was a representative for a pharmaceuticals company based in Nottingham and had a heart for homeless people. Jo was a palliative care nurse working in a hospice in the Home Counties. Her younger sister had died from cancer when she was 24 and Jo had a special concern to support the families of patients with cancer. Kwame was a financial consultant from Ghana, living in South London and passionate about football. He not only saw the home matches of his beloved Chelsea but travelled to a majority of their away games. Rachel was a dress designer from Liverpool and had met all the 'big names' in the rag trade. She was a new Christian and hoping to find more life and fun on the houseparty than she had encountered in the traditional church where she was worshipping. Steve was a computer programmer from South Wales. His father was an Elim pastor and Steve had rebelled against his parents' spiritual and moral values during his teens. Now looking for a spiritual home where he would be comfortable, Steve was relieved to be with a group of people who knew nothing about his past.

Becky had lived in Ballymena, Northern Ireland, until she left school to study at an English University. She was now working for a television production company in Manchester and made quite an entrance when she arrived on her beloved Honda Fireblade motorbike. James had studied medicine at Cambridge and was working in a London hospital. His long term ambition was to get a consultant's position in an A & E Department but his close friends said he had a real gift for Bible teaching and should be considering the Christian ministry. Jane was a part-time teacher living in Truro. She had previously worked full time in a school in inner-city Bristol but was taking time out in rural Cornwall. She missed the multicultural vibrancy of her former church fellowship and felt it would not be long before she returned to an urban environment.

I have conducted numerous houseparties where I have met this broad cross section of God's family. There is sufficient diversity when a group of Christians describe where they live, what they do and their passions in life. But if you add to this mix their doctrinal emphases, denominational backgrounds, worship preferences and personality types, then deep differences will emerge.

It may seem a slender principle with which to begin a book on uniting the tribes of evangelicalism but it is a foundational truth. Those who have confessed Jesus is

Lord and believe in their heart that God raised Jesus from the dead (Rom. 10:9–10) are 'all one in Christ Jesus' (Gal. 3:28). One way to understand the phrase 'All one in Christ Jesus' is 'You are *one person* in Christ Jesus.' In most parts of the world differences are made to matter and diversity is a major barrier to uniting people. The uniqueness of the Christian family is that our unity is grounded in diversity. Humanly speaking, Christians in the UK are an incredibly diverse group of people, but if you add to this the membership of God's family in scores of nations, you have diversity with a capital D! But in Jesus Christ, this multi-coloured diversity is focused exclusively on the one who by his sacrifice has made our amazing unity possible.

There are three key areas which for centuries have been flash points for divisions between people. Society has frequently made differences matter when it comes to ethnic background, social class and gender. History teaches us that racial prejudice, unjust class divisions and the subjugation of women have been the cause of violence and civil unrest.

The unique message of those who are 'all one in Christ Jesus' is 'There is neither Jew not Greek, slave nor free, male nor female' (Gal. 3:28). Differences are not meant to matter when it comes to membership in God's family. Whatever our ethnic background, social status or gender, if we have been saved by faith in Christ, we have been born again into a new family. God is our heavenly Father and we are his children: all believers in Christ are united as brothers and sisters in the one family. The point to note in this passage from Galatians is that the world made differences matter in the first century and this attitude was marring the full potential of experiencing the diverse unity that God had planned for his family. Jesus Christ, by his atoning death and mighty resurrection, has inaugurated a new family which renders null and void the differences which the world says matter. Leon Morris draws attention to the world-shattering claim in these verses. Paul is *not* writing about a humanly engineered unity: 'He is saying that when people are saved by Jesus Christ they are brought into a marvellous unity, a unity between the saved and the Saviour and a unity that binds together all the saved. Even the major divisions in the human race cannot do away with this unity.'[1]

The message of Galatians is plain. Guard this unique unity you have in Christ. In our concern to defend the truth of the gospel and the purity of the church, we can be tempted to introduce 'add-ons' to the faith. God says membership in his family is based on trusting 'In Christ alone, by grace alone, through faith alone.' When we say this principle is insufficient and insist on further proofs, such as precisely defining aspects of doctrine and lifestyle, then we are in danger of lapsing into legalism as a basis for relating and going beyond Scripture which says we are to accept one another as Christ has accepted us (Rom.15:7).

There are important issues on which Christians disagree. But must there be full agreement on all matters of doctrine before we can extend the hand of fellowship? It is suggested that the following are some of the issues which currently divide evangelicals . . .[2]

- Creation – how the world began
- Eschatology – the second coming of Christ and the end of the world
- Atonement – aspects of the doctrine of the cross
- Women – are women permitted to have a teaching or leadership role in the church, or prohibited from doing so?

- Gifts of the Spirit – are all of the gifts listed in the New Testament ones which should be exercised in the church of today?
- Hell – are the lost destined for eternal conscious punishment?
- Mission – the relationship between evangelism, social action and political protest
- Israel – how we respond to the modern nation of Israel and God's future plans for the Jews
- Scripture – the infallibility and interpretation of the Bible
- Sexuality – how do we respond to the Bible's teaching about heterosexual cohabiting and homosexual acts?
- War – is there such a thing as a just war or is the way of Jesus always pacifism?

No one doubts the seriousness of these issues. But do I have to check that the views of another Christian are totally in accord with my views before I can accept them as a believer? Or am I prepared to stand on the principle that those who have been saved by Jesus Christ are all one in him? There is a unity between the saved and the Saviour and a unity that binds together all the saved.

There is serious diversity among us. There are opposing views on important matters of doctrine. We feel the sharp pain of disagreement. But the Lord has given us the inestimable privilege of being 'all one in Christ Jesus' and this is the sole starting place for our unity.

Questions

1. Look around your own church fellowship. What are the issues that create tensions among the members? How are differences resolved?

2. What is your experience of mixing with Christians from different evangelical communities? Has it been positive or negative?
3. Do you consider Galatians 3:27–28 a sufficient basis for spiritual unity? Are there other scriptures you would want to add for consideration?

Books

Steve Brady, *All You Need is Christ* (Milton Keynes: Authentic, 2007).

Timothy George (editor), *Pilgrims on the Sawdust Trail: Evangelical Ecumenism and the Quest for Christian Identity* (Grand Rapids Michigan: Baker Academic, 2004).

John Stott, *Evangelical Truth: A Personal Plea for Unity* (Leicester: IVP, 1999).

Chapter Two

Why evangelical unity matters

Given that evangelicals will always have their differences – sometimes serious to breaking point – why do we need to lay stress on evangelical unity? Is it not more desirable that when we reach a point where serious differences are damaging us spiritually and emotionally, we agree to a separation?

I fear that currently in the evangelical world we are reliving Paul and Barnabas's experience of sharp disagreement which led to a parting of the ways (Acts 15:36–40). But note this Scripture passage is not a mandate for division: rather it is an encouragement to strive even more for the unity of the gospel in the bonds of peace.

I suggest there are six reasons why evangelical unity matters:

1. The truth of the gospel

Our unity is intended to be a witness to the truth of the gospel. Those who profess they are saved by faith through grace are made one family in him. Through our unity we provide a visual aid of the reconciling power of the gospel. Jesus Christ broke down the walls of partition that divided us from God and each other and, by his death, reconciled us to himself. Jesus by his death also healed our divisions and abolished the human barriers that separate people from each other.

2. God's intentions for his family

God intends his family to enjoy close fellowship with each other. We should not learn about each other through third and fourth hand opinions. Differences of emphasis and deep disagreements have always been a feature among evangelicals but we have neglected to our cost the value of meeting with those with whom we have the deepest disagreements. Our Pharisaic attitudes are a poor witness to the unity that God wants, as is our speaking of other family members in a graceless tone. We need a greater sense that when we diminish another family member, we are in grave danger of denigrating the work of Jesus in their life. Being rejected by the body of Christ always deeply damages Christians.

It is interesting to see the common features between the ways we relate as evangelicals and the political systems of countries I visit. Wherever there is persecution of the church by a despotic state, there is always a clear process that is followed. Firstly, there is disinformation through the media outlets, then denigration of leaders which seeks to discredit their character, and finally the process of discrimination which deliberately marginalises. Some may find this a distasteful and inappropriate analogy, but I find this same pattern of disinformation, denigration and discrimination in parts of the evangelical world. It is a dreadful stain on our Christian witness and needs to be addressed.

3. Tribal gatherings exclude people

We are diminished when we choose to meet only members of our tribe. One of the most damaging features of evangelical life is our structured gatherings which one of my friends has described as: 'hermetically sealed communities where we only meet with those we broadly agree with'. We are more comfortable meeting in conferences with people who do things our way. Some conference organisers aim for the highest common denominator when issuing invitations to speakers – if you can tick all our boxes then you can grace our platform.

It is worth noting that the Keswick Convention has historically been committed to an open platform which welcomes all evangelicals and this value was reaffirmed in the position statement of 2000

> We wish to occupy evangelical centre ground, warmly welcoming all evangelical 'tribes', with a generosity of spirit in this regard and no narrowing of our position to define ourselves within the evangelical constituency. We note that many events and conferences are becoming increasingly sectionalised, and we would want Keswick genuinely to sustain its breadth of involvement with evangelicals as a whole. The range of speakers, worship, music and programme style should therefore reflect appropriate diversity, in line with our primary purposes as a Convention.[3]

4. Evangelical core commitments

If we meet in what Os Guinness calls our 'enclaves of separateness' then we lack a broad forum to debate the substantive issues of the day. It is a matter of urgency that we create an ongoing forum to come up with a definition of one of the major issues facing us: What is an evangelical? Will this be a 'tribal' theological description which will simultaneously include and exclude? Will we be open to both traditional and progressive ways of describing evangelical identity? Such a forum would provide space to debate some of the most divisive issues. What is lacking between the tribes at present is agreement about core evangelical commitments. We need to find ways of articulating what is primary and what is secondary. In which areas may we exercise legitimate plurality? How do we interact graciously with those we differ from doctrinally? There need to be ground rules for articulating our differences graciously. These debates need to take place in a forum which includes all the tribes.

5. Local pressures

Our national disunity places pastoral pressures on the local church. The national and international debates among evangelicals are influential in the life of the local church. Tapes from the ministry of Keswick, Spring Harvest, New Word Alive, New Wine, Proclamation Trust, church.co.uk are freely shared among the home-groups of dozens of local churches. Sharing in the local church is a natural part of life together in a local fellowship and linking with a national conference can be the means of spiritual blessing. The danger comes when there are subtle pressures to conform to a particular pattern of doctrinal teaching with no freedom to dissent. Under the influence of a national movement, we can become more guarded in expressing fellowship with local believers, and expressions of local unity can be weakened as a result. We can end up feeling a greater loyalty to a national movement that defines and speaks more clearly for us, than we do to the local expression of unity.

6. The spiritual needs of the world

The spiritual needs of the world command a greater unity. Our disunity weakens the potential for thoughtful and effective evangelism in the UK. Unquestionably, the greatest challenge facing all the UK churches is how we reach a new generation of citizens with the good news of Jesus Christ. Traditionally, evangelistic initiatives have been the strongest contribution the evangelical movement has made to the British church scene. It was the zeal and vision of evangelicals which lay behind the initial invitation to Billy Graham, whose ministry in the 1950s-1980s brought thousands to Christ. Only later did the wider church back this initiative.

Linking unity with evangelism corresponds with the emphasis Jesus gave to his disciples and the indivisible relationship between the unity of disciples and their effective mission. We need to reflect seriously on the words of Jesus: 'By this all men will know that you are my disciples, if you love one another' (John 13:35) and his prayer that his disciples would be brought to complete unity 'to let the world know that you sent me and have loved them even as you have loved me' (John 17:23). Jesus emphasised unity and evangelism when he spoke of the disciples's unity and the effectiveness of their mission. It applies just as much to us.

These are gospel commands and presumably, where there is a failure in obedience, we are allowing our divisions to say to the world 'We hate each other.' This is a sinful disobedience by the church which carries a high penalty in a world starved of gospel knowledge and kingdom power.

In the rest of the chapters, I want to explore in greater depth the foundations of our evangelical unity and the practical steps we can take to handle our differences without destroying our unity.

In summary, I suggest this is the challenge for evangelicals who are serious about unity

- For the sake of our unity in truth, are we able to bring a greater focus on our areas of common agreement?
- Are we willing to discover how the insights given to part of the body can become insights shared with the whole?
- Have we the capacity to recognise the authentic truth of Christianity, especially when it is expressed in an unfamiliar vocabulary?
- Can we ask the Lord to make us less defensive about our traditions and more critical of our innovations?

Questions

1. Is 'evangelical unity' on the agenda for Christian churches? Is it a topic that is discussed in your local church? Would you be willing to raise it for consideration at a church gathering?
2. Evangelicals are often accused of being intolerant towards other evangelicals because they appear to find doctrinal deficiencies in others. How do you

understand the teaching of Jesus in Matthew 7:1–6 about such behaviour?

3. Are evangelicals really in 'tribal communities' or is this down to the imagination of Christian writers? If it is true that we are 'tribal' how do you most categorize people spiritually?

Books

Michael A.G. Haykins and Kenneth J. Stewart (eds.), *The Emergence of Evangelicalism* (Nottingham: IVP, 2008).

Timothy Larsen and Daniel J.Treier (eds.), *The Cambridge Companion to Evangelical Theology* (Cambridge: CUP, 2007).

Alister McGrath, *Evangelicalism and the Future of Christianity* (Downers Grove Illinois: IVP, 1995).

Bruce Milne, *Dynamic Diversity: The New Humanity Church for Today and Tomorrow* (Nottingham: IVP, 2006).

Chapter Three

Evangelicals fragmented

If 'All one in Christ' is historically a core value for evangelicals, why is it that the evangelical movement appears to be hopelessly fragmented?

Rob Warner chooses 1966 as a watershed moment for English evangelicals. This was the year when the two foremost evangelicals of the time, Martyn Lloyd-Jones and John Stott, had a public disagreement and pan-evangelical confidence collapsed. Warner suggests this was also the moment when two distinct emphases emerged which ended the existing coalition of evangelicalism. He describes the first emphasis as 'entrepreneurial' because it spawned a movement full of visionary ideas and mission initiative. It drew its support largely from the growing charismatic constituency of the late 1970s which was focused on a revived Evangelical Alliance under the leadership of Clive Calver and the Easter conference – Spring Harvest. It particularly emphasised the life-changing aspects of the gospel and the call of God to be active in mission. There was a recovery of the evangelical prophetic tradition of public campaigning for social changes.

The other emphasis was more focused on biblical and doctrinal evangelical identity, with a particular stress on Reformed teaching and theological enquiry.[4] There was a suspicion of spiritual experience which was not rooted in biblical teaching and a concern that the priority of evangelism suffered if mission included social action. This found a focus in such places as the Banner of Truth conferences, the British Evangelical Council (now called Affinity) and the Evangelical Ministry assembly.

One of the most public debates for the Church of England in recent times has been who speaks for evangelical Anglicans. The Church of England Evangelical Council traditionally has been a focal point for the unity of all the 'tribes' of evangelical Anglicans, but the recent global debates on human sexuality have marred this unity. Evangelicals in the Church of England now have at least four main groupings where they can choose to gather with other like-minded members: Anglican Mainstream, Reform, Fulcrum and the New Wine Network.

Other recent trends which could lead to a further opening up of divides among evangelicals in all denominations include the growth of interest in Reformed theology. Dave Roberts, in a *Christianity* magazine, article says we need to be careful about labelling evangelicals – 'but there seems to be a seismic change under way in British evangelicalism. The charismatic impulse is no longer defining the agenda of evangelicals.'[5]

The charismatic impulse certainly came to the fore when Todd Bentley's US-based *Fresh Fire Ministries* hit the headlines in 2007-08 and it opened an interesting debate among charismatic leaders. Terry Virgo, leader of New Frontiers International, wrote two expansive pieces on his blog, offering cautious negatives about the manifestations witnessed in Todd Bentley's ministry and, at the same time, highlighting sound historical examples from the history of Revival movements.[6] Rob White, part of the leadership team in Baptist Mainstream, offered helpful guidelines on how to respond to what was happening through Todd Bentley's ministry

> Keep as open a mind & heart as possible, without ignoring your spiritual antennae. We need to keep perspective on these things, realising that there is almost a default fascination with trends, fashions & technique, which are strong features of our wider culture, especially at the moment. However, when (and only when) we sense that there is a wave of God breaking, should we seek to go to Florida.[7]

Former minister of Westminster Chapel, R.T. Kendall, was less than sympathetic to Todd Bentley and his Lakeland Florida ministry. He says it took a little bit of courage for him to endorse the Toronto Blessing in 1994 and he has never regretted this but he was going to take even more courage to say that the Lakeland phenomenon was not of God. He eventually went public with his opposition

> First, never once have I heard a clear message of the Gospel of Jesus Christ from the Lakeland platform – except when a guest speaker did it. Second, when people were being baptized in the name of the Father, the Son and 'Bam – bam', it both trivialized the Trinity and baptism itself. This is serious, serious trivializing. Third, if you were to ask how much a fear of God and conviction of sin emanated from these services – on a scale of 1 to 100 – I would say zero. It comes to this: is the Bible true? Because I believe the Bible I can testify: the jury of my mind on Lakeland is in. Leave Lakeland alone.[8]

Subsequent to these comments, Todd Bentley was suspended because of inappropriate behaviour with a member of his congregation, which confirmed some evangelicals in their view of the unsound nature of the ministry from Lakeland. They wondered why the warning signs were not flagged up earlier by pentecostals and questioned the gullible openness that often characterises a response to 'revival' phenomena. The different responses to such events serve to widen the gulf between the tribes.

In a recent magazine article, Andy Peck identifies seven tribes of evangelicalism and, after examining their characteristics, considers the negative impact this tribalism has had on church unity.[9] His article includes the views of a range of evangelical leaders. Nick Baines, the Bishop of Croydon, suggests: 'Evangelicalism has become distinctive for its defensiveness, working out who is in and who is out. Its gift to the world seems to have been fragmentation.' Joel Edwards, the former General Director of the Evangelical Alliance, reckons 'Ninety per cent of our differences in the EA have been about mission.' Local church leader Dave Roberts says disagreement does not need to be divisive: 'We need to think more about our theology and be prepared to stand for what we believe within our particular grouping. Burying differences can blunt our cutting edge. What matters is that we can be gracious to those who disagree with us.'

Evangelical unity is a good theme for a book in the 'Keswick Foundation' series in any year but right now it appears topical and urgent. Unity among evangelicals has never been as threatened as it is now, with the apparent divisions that have developed over the last decade.

Evangelicals are losing the ground that we gained in the 1970s and 1980s when we honoured and accepted

one another with greater grace across the denominational and organisational divisions. It grieves my
spirit that evangelicals cannot find a greater gospel
unity, and I fear we are in grave danger of missing the
fullest expression of evangelical cooperation to face the
demanding missionary opportunities here in the UK.

When I wrote the book *Build that Bridge*[10] over twenty
years ago, I spoke of an evangelical culture where I
sensed that differences were overstressed; where there
was a hardening of attitudes; where suspicion was rife
and ghetto fellowship the norm for many believers. I
described a scenario which, with regret, I have updated

- A is suspicious of B because B goes to Spring Harvest
  and reads Third Way.
- B is suspicious of A because A attends New Word
  Alive and reads the *Evangelicals Now* newspaper.
- C is suspicious of D because D has been to a conference on the dangers of Open Theism theology and
  finds it intellectually stimulating to debate the classic
  differences between Calvinism and Arminianism.
- D is suspicious of C and refutes the charge he is stuck
  in a sixteenth century time warp. He doubts that C
  should even call himself an evangelical and his annual
  attendance at Greenbelt and his love of Iona music confirm his place is outside the evangelical camp.
- E and F were regular prayer partners in the local ministers' gathering in their town but they have not spoken
  to each other since F decided to call an ordained
  woman minister to join his church's leadership team. E
  is implacably opposed to the ordination of women and
  judges F to have been unfaithful to gospel teaching.
- G is suspicious of H because H refused to sign a
  Christian Union statement of faith which used the
  phrase 'infallibility' in the section on the Bible.

- H believes G has been corrupted by a fundamentalist ideology which teaches people how to read the Bible.

I accept that when it comes to the interpretation of biblical truth, differences do matter and deep issues of conscience must be addressed. It is, however, unacceptable and contrary to scriptural unity that we appear no longer to meet, talk and debate our differences.

Evangelical unity has always been a fragile part of our identity and we have been more diverse than we are prepared to acknowledge. Theological tribes are much more complex than appears and there has always been disagreement on a range of issues. But in our diversity, we have always affirmed that our unity is more important than our disagreements. We have symbolised this unity through our support for the Evangelical Alliance and national initiatives such as CARE, Care for the Family and the international ministry of Tear Fund.

For all the plethora of national conferences there is no one place where we can hear a range of evangelical voices. We have deepened the tribal identities by inviting speakers who are carefully chosen to reflect the emphasis of the organisation. Ten years ago there would be a number of speakers whose ministry was accepted across the tribal divides. It is a sign of the times that today there are only a handful of speakers who could unite evangelicals in a conference. Similarly there is a lack of Christian journals read by the whole constituency and constructively critical of evangelical life. We have succumbed to 'talking up' an event without critical evaluation. Whatever our tribal affiliation, this lack of critical yet affirming evaluation needs to be acknowledged.

We attend our tribal conferences, read our tribal newspapers and listen to tapes by our tribal leaders and all the time the challenge of Acts 15 is avoided. The Jerusalem gathering was a defining moment in the life of the early church when differences where brought out into the open and the believers were seen to be making 'every effort to keep the unity of the Spirit through the bond of peace' (Eph. 4:3).

Our Acts 15 moment has arrived. It just needs someone to send out the invitations.

Questions

1. Why do you think evangelicals are so fragmented in the United Kingdom today?
2. Read through the A-H list on page 20 and find where you may be in the mix. What steps do you think leaders and churches can take to work closer with other evangelical networks?
3. Research the different evangelical churches within a five mile radius with the possibility of establishing some kind of link with those churches. This could be done through a team who could:

   - write/email for some information
   - visit a church/churches
   - establish relational contacts
   - find out about prayer needs
   - invite people to attend a coffee morning etc.

List some other ways in which there could be greater cooperation between congregations.

Books

Craig Bartholomew, Robin Parry and Andrew West (eds), *The Futures of Evangelicalism: Issues and Prospects* (Leicester: IVP, 2003).

Steven Croft, *Transforming Communities: Reimagining the Church for the 21st Century* (London: DLT, 2002).

Iain H. Murray, *Evangelicalism Divided: A Record of Crucial Change in the Years 1950–2000* (Edinburgh: Banner of Truth Trust, 2000).

Rob Warner, *Reinventing English Evangelicalism: 1966–2001* (Milton Keynes: Paternoster, 2007).

Part two

The essentials of unity

Chapter 4

Bind us together

In a church I was pastoring, I remember glancing round the congregation during the offering one Sunday and being overwhelmed by the diversity of God's family worshipping under one roof. I saw

- A gardener from a local hotel
- A discharged prisoner from a local jail
- A man who had rowed the Atlantic Ocean
- A woman who had nursed with Florence Nightingale
- An authoress with two books to her name
- A window-cleaner
- Two itinerant Bible teachers
- Five doctors and two hospital porters
- An ex-professional footballer
- A family from Alaska running a nursing home
- A missionary family en route to Africa
- Five single parent families
- A long distance lorry driver
- A member of Cliff Richard's backing group
- A black belt in judo . . .

At this point I had to stop counting as it was time for the offertory prayer! Take a long look at the Christians you know and you will discover there are dozens of reasons why diverse groups of believers might be expected to quarrel and divide. But we are members in *one* family, which is why we now consider what it is that binds us together in the unity we have in Jesus Christ.

At the heart of our life together is a 'sharing in' fellowship with the Father, the Son and the Holy Spirit. This is our life. This is our secret. With God's help, we have to work to establish meaningful fellowship with other believers. Without the work of the Holy Trinity, there can be no fellowship in the church. Without the active participation of a community of believers, God's intentions for his church are never realised.

The meaning of the Greek word *koinonia*, which is translated in our Bibles as fellowship, has a double edge to it. *Koinonia* is 'having a share with someone in something' but this one word also carries the meaning of both 'sharing in' and 'sharing out'. Because of our trusting faith in Jesus Christ, we have a share in nothing less than fellowship with the Holy Trinity.

Fellowship with the Trinity

Sharing in the life of the Trinity is a fruit of our new birth. We have fellowship with God the Father by sharing in his life (1 John 1:3–6); we have fellowship with God the Son by sharing through faith in his broken body and his shed blood (1 Cor. 10:16–17) and we have fellowship with the Holy Spirit by sharing in his life and he enables us to enjoy our salvation and serve in spite of our weakness (2 Cor. 13:4). This unity is explicitly centred on Jesus

Christ and a Christian is united to each phase of Christ's redeeming work

- We share with Jesus a flesh and blood humanity which is why we can name Jesus as our elder brother (Heb. 2:11–15).
- We share by faith in the death of Jesus on the cross and this produces such a close unity of relationship we can say 'I no longer live, but Christ lives in me' (Gal. 2:20).
- We share in the resurrection life of Jesus and this not only gives our life new directions, it is a pledge of our own bodily resurrection (1 Cor. 15:12–58; Col. 3:1).
- We share in the work of the ministry of the Holy Spirit who makes Christ real to us and in us and empowers our living with God's gifts (Acts 1:8; Eph. 5:18; Rom. 12:4–13).
- We share in the missionary calling of Christ to expand the Kingdom of God and build the church of God (Mk. 1:15; Matt. 16:18; Matt. 28:19–20).
- We share in the present reign of Jesus in glory (2 Tim. 2:11).
- We share in the riches of the inheritance which is in Jesus (Rom. 8:17).
- We have the promise of sharing ultimately in the triumphant reign of the Lord Jesus Christ in glory (Col. 3:4).
- We have been admitted by our new birth into the *koinonia* of the Trinity and are entitled to enjoy fully the privileges of 'the grace of our Lord Jesus Christ, and the love of God and the fellowship of the Holy Spirit' (2 Cor. 13:14).

This is the quality of spiritual life which Christians have in common and focusing on these aspects of life together leads to a deepening of fellowship. When we bypass these foundational aspects of fellowship and instead focus on the differences between 'us' and 'them' we never experience the rich relationships God intended for his family.

This rich 'sharing in' should naturally lead to an overflow of 'sharing out' in fellowship with others that is costly, loving, faith building and persevering. This quality of fellowship is nothing less than the overflow of the life of the Trinity in our own lives. We only love each other because God first loved us. We serve each other because our servant Leader showed us the way when he washed the feet of the disciples. We persevere with each other because our Saviour persevered all the way to the cross for us.

Instant friendship: no basis for deep fellowship

In our relationships with other Christians there are factors which can enable 'instant' friendship. It might be a shared outlook (the Bach Cantata Pilgrimage with John Eliot Gardiner or the jazz pianist Diana Krall's album *Quiet Nights*); a compatible temperament (early riser or night owl); common experiences (cruise ship to Alaska or visiting the art galleries of Florence); same age group (enjoying grandchildren or a gap year in Africa); quirky passions (Everton Football Club or the Edward Elgar Society).

It is this dimension of compatible interests which can enhance friendships but it can *never* be the basis for deep fellowship. True fellowship must have a stronger foundation than shared interests. Firstly, this is because when the storms of disagreement begin to batter the house, our mutual love for a Bach cantata or jazz by Diana Krall will not be strong enough to keep us together. Secondly, if we only have 'fellowship' with those with whom we feel an instant affinity, then we may as well adjourn to the nearest telephone box for fellowship with like-minded people. I say 'telephone box' because basing fellowship on the principle of 'we must be in total agreement on everything' guarantees shrinking of fellowship. We will eventually discover there is something that we don't have in common and the membership of the fellowship will become smaller and smaller, until there are just two of us left in the fellowship circle and I am not too sure about you!

There is a well known story which illustrates the dangers of narrow fellowship

> Once I saw this guy on a bridge about to jump. I said 'Don't do it!' He said 'Nobody loves me.' I said 'God loves you. Do you believe in God?'
>
> He said 'Yes.' I said 'Are you a Christian or a Jew?' He said 'A Christian.' I said, 'Me, too! Protestant or Catholic?' He said 'Protestant.' I said 'Me, too! What franchise?' He said 'Baptist.' I said 'Me, too! Northern Baptist or Southern Baptist?' He said 'Northern Baptist.' I said 'Me, too! Northern Conservative Baptist or Northern Liberal Baptist?'
>
> He said 'Northern Conservative Baptist.' I said 'Me, too! Northern Conservative Baptist Great Lakes Region, or Northern Conservative Baptist Eastern Region?' He said 'Northern Conservative Baptist Great Lakes Region.' I said 'Me, too! Northern Conservative Baptist Great Lakes Region Council of 1879, or Northern Conservative Baptist Great Lakes Region Council of 1912?' He said 'Northern Conservative Baptist Great Lakes Region Council of 1912.' I said 'Die, heretic!' And I pushed him over.

This is a caricature of what is a sad reality in many parts of the Christian world. It is what I term pseudo-fellowship because it dishonours the wonderful doctrine of the unity of God's people. Point me to that passage in the Bible which says we can only have fellowship with those who totally agree with us on i) how the world began ii) which version of the Bible is reliable iii) which doctrinal basis is sound iv) what conferences are safe to attend v) what books I must have in my library vi) which Christian authors must never be cited in conservative company. If these are the criteria for sharing together, then inevitably we narrow down the rich potential of fellowship. More seriously, we grieve the Spirit of God (Eph. 4:30).

Building fellowship principles

The creation of fellowship is not something that happens automatically. Fellowship has to be worked at, especially with those we don't have an instant affinity with. There are some basic working principles which can motivate us to experience the quality of life together God has planned for the family.

- We may not have much in common with another believer, but we are in grave danger when we dismissively say 'They are just not my sort of person.' If Jesus has made his home in someone's life then we have to extend the hospitality of the heart toward them.
- We may deeply dislike another believer because their attitudes anger us, but we must remember they too have been brought into the family of God by the Saviour, who loved us unconditionally while we were sinners (Rom. 5:8).

- We may be tempted to doubt someone is a 'true' Christian because their lifestyle is extravagant and self indulgent, but we must remember the test of fellowship is how they relate to Jesus (1 John 4:15).
- We may find it difficult to forgive someone for acts of injustice and wrong doing. This lack of a forgiving spirit can sometimes be towards a whole membership of believers. But we must remember the principle of walking in the light and confessing our sins before the Lord (1 John 1:5–10). For serious breaches of fellowship life, we may need to reach out and ask others to help us in a mediation process.

It is normal to experience the brokenness of fellowship occasionally – but by submitting to God's help, our brokenness can be mended. What is abnormal is the ignoring of broken relationships and walking away from the scenes of destruction which can be so deeply damaging to fellowship life.

God created us to be the healthy body of Christ and each part of the body is intended to work in harmonious partnership with the rest (1 Cor. 12:12). It is a serious moment when the eye says to the hand, 'I don't need you.' It is impossible for the body to function in the way God intended when we cut off a member and say 'You are not needed' (1 Cor. 12:21).

Halting the drift towards disunity

Paul felt the danger of drifting towards disunity and division when he wrote his letter to the Philippians. He obviously enjoyed a warm and close relationship with this young church and their fellowship was a great joy to him (Phil. 1:3–9). But if there was any defect in this church, it was their lack of care in guarding the unity of their fellowship. There are hints of relationship problems (4:2) and some in the church may have believed they had 'arrived' spiritually and felt superior to other believers. This spirit of pride needed countering, so Paul serves as a wise pastor by anticipating the dangers of a greater disunity developing (3:2–4).

Philippians 2 is one of the greatest passages of the New Testament and sets forth the example of Jesus Christ as the only reliable foundation for any unity between believers. In its opening verses, Paul explains that because we are members of the same spiritual family, we have inherited a family DNA. This inherited DNA needs guarding and preserving and must never be taken for granted. Unity may be a natural fruit of the gospel but it does not come 'naturally' to our relationships. In the opening verse of the chapter, Paul reminds his friends of four wonderful benefits they have received since becoming followers of Jesus which may be summarised in a series of questions (2:1)

- Have you received any *encouragement* from being united to Christ?
- Have you received any *comfort* from knowing the love of Christ?
- Have you benefited as a church from the *fellowship* you enjoy in the Holy Spirit?
- Are your lives richer from experiencing the *compassion* of your Heavenly Father?

Paul knows the Philippi church can give a resounding 'Yes and amen' to these questions, so he suggests they make his pastoral heart overflow with joy (2:2) by revealing these same Christlike qualities towards each other. The attitude of Jesus Christ to each of us should become our Christlike attitude to other believers

- Be a constant encouragement
- Be a comforting companion
- Be open-handed in fellowship
- Be open-hearted with compassion

We should grasp the huge potential of what it means to be bound together in Christ.

- In our relating to Christ we have the potential to be of *one mind* with other believers (v2). This does not imply group thinking of the mindless variety where we leave someone else to do our thinking for us and blindly follow like sheep. It does mean cultivating a disposition which seeks to harmonise creatively with other disciples of Jesus Christ.
- In our relating to Christ, we have the possibility of sharing *one love* (v2). This is not to be confused with that natural affinity which makes no demands. Paul is referring to *agape* love for which we need the strength of the Holy Spirit. The essential nature of *agape* loving is unpacked in Matthew 5.43–48, where God is seen to be benevolent to people whether they are friend or foe.
- In our relating to Christ, we share the *one life* which Paul terms 'being one in spirit and purpose' (v2). The quality of our relationships should be characterised by humility and consideration of others. We are to spotlight the excellent gifts and potential of others and allow our own interests to take a backseat (2:3–4).

Looking to the interests of others

The pinnacle of Paul's argument is displayed in verses 5–11 which, F.B. Meyer suggests, is a paragraph which

stands in 'almost unapproachable and unexampled
majesty' in the whole of the Bible. If humility and consideration of others is the character of Christian fellowship, then Christ Jesus exemplifies par excellence the
disposition of 'looking to the interests of others.' Look at
the words of this worship song (Phil. 2:6–11) and consider the pastoral challenges it poses to any group of
believers serious about the deepening of their fellowship.

If we are earnest in our desire to look to the interests
of others and do everything without complaining or
arguing, then our life of service should be shaped by
what Jesus was prepared to do. The mind that motivated Christ must be the mind of each believer.

- Before Bethlehem, Jesus shared with the Father the
  glory of heaven, and had done so since before the
  world began. But Jesus never considered this equality
  with God something to be held onto at all costs.
- At Bethlehem, the one who had inhabited the place of
  perfection was born in a borrowed stable. He who
  experienced the security of heaven became exposed to
  the risk of vulnerability and rejection.
- In the Upper Room, he was the servant. When everyone else was quarrelling about status, it was Jesus
  who took the towel and basin and washed their feet.
- On the cross at Calvary, he hung helplessly and bore
  the ignominy of the shame and suffering for our sin.
  In those oft-quoted words, it was those hands that
  had flung stars into space that were surrendered to
  cruel nails.
- God has exalted Jesus and given him the highest status in the universe. Our proudest titles and positions
  are nothing compared to Jesus, who is the Name
  above all names.

Those who are serious in their devotion to Jesus will be devoted to a serious fellowship with other believers.

Questions

1. If 1 Corinthians 12:14–31 is a picture of the body life God intends for his family, how can it be achieved locally and globally? What steps need to be taken in order to foster such a meaningful way of relating together?
2. What things could your local church do beyond regular worship services to deepen spiritual unity throughout the congregation?

Books

Eddie Gibbs and Ian Coffey, *Church Next: Quantum Changes in Christian Ministry* (Leicester: IVP, 2001).

Phil Potter, *The Challenge of Change – A Guide to Shaping Change and Changing the Shape of the Church* (Oxford: BRF, 2009).

Ian Stackhouse, *The Gospel-Driven Church: Retrieving Classical Ministry for Contemporary Revivalism* (Milton Keynes: Paternoster, 2004).

Chapter 5

Primary and secondary truth

If gospel unity does not imply we have to agree on absolutely everything when it comes to doctrine, then who decides between essentials and non-essentials? What is primary and what is secondary truth, in deciding a basis for working with other Christians, and who is the arbiter for making these decisions? We often lack the fullest expression of evangelical unity because we believe falsely that we can only enjoy fellowship with those who are like-minded believers with us, *in every aspect of Christian truth*.

It might help to distinguish between primary and secondary truth to take a short test of judgment with the following 24 questions. The process of choosing where you make your spiritual home is important and will involve exploring the core doctrinal statements and vision documents of a local church.

Imagine you have visited a range of church websites and read the following statements. In a checklist of priorities of what you expect from an evangelical church, consider and mark each item with a P for primary truth or S for secondary truth:

Checklist of priorities

1. We hold orthodox Christian beliefs, subscribing to the historical creeds which speak of our belief in God as Father, Son and Holy Spirit as well as the great Reformation principles of 'Christ Alone, Scripture Alone, Faith Alone.'

2. We are members of the Evangelical Alliance and we subscribe to their Basis of Faith which you can find at www.eauk.org/about/basis-of-faith.cfm.

3. We believe in the divine inspiration, infallibility and inerrancy of the Bible as originally given and as such it is the supreme and final authority for what we believe and how we live our life together.

4. The stated mission vision of this church is to go Christ's way and make disciples of Jesus.

5. Our desire is to see churches that are built on New Testament principles through receiving the Ephesians 4 ministries, where the word of God is honoured and there is openness to the work of the Holy Spirit. We believe in a restored church and embrace Haggai's promise that 'The latter glory of this house will be greater than the former.'

A closer examination of these churches reveals the following facts:

6. The ministry team includes an ordained woman who preaches regularly.

7. The government of the church appears to be a group of elders appointed by the pastor with no consultation with the wider church.

8. The church Meeting meets monthly 'to discern God's will for our life together.' The church clearly states 'Under Christ the church Meeting is

the final authority for the church's mission and ministry.'

9.   The church believes in the 'priesthood of all believers. Every member has been gifted by God's Spirit and has a role to play in the life of the church. In particular, every member is called to witness to the Good News of Jesus.'

10. Baptism is open for both infants and adult believers.

11. There is no obvious church policy on divorce and remarriage and same sex civil partnerships.

12. The local Masonic group hires the church for an annual carol service.

13. The church is a full member of local Churches Together which includes Roman Catholics.

14. Spiritual gifts are encouraged in public worship, including speaking in tongues, sharing picture visions and words of prophetic knowledge.

15. The Lord's Supper is observed twice monthly but friends who worship in this church have observed the minister uses a prayer of blessing over the bread and wine and uses the emphatic language 'This *is* the body of Christ' and 'This *is* the blood of Christ.'

16. The church youth club is known to show category 18 films on Saturday nights and there is no ban on serving alcohol on the premises.

17. The church is even-handed in its approach to the politics of the Middle East and believes in a two-state solution for the conflict between Israel and Palestine.

18. One of the elders is a passionate creationist and in open conflict with the school where he teaches.

19. Because of its active social ministries to the community, the church has nearly a thousand people on its premises during the week but there is an apparent lack of evangelistic strategy for sharing the gospel with this core fringe.

20. There is a well-attended early morning prayer meeting each week and a programme for prayer triplets.
21. There are regular Alpha courses, using the original material from Holy Trinity Brompton, and a residential Holy Spirit weekend.
22. The church is more comfortable with the Christianity Explored course as it 'resonates with our overall vision and core values'.
23. Each year the church takes a party to Spring Harvest/New Word Alive/New Wine/Keswick/ Centre Parcs/ (Please tick any or all).
24. The preferred Bible version in the church is New King James/New International/English Standard Version/Good News.

If you have marked all 24 answers with a 'P', I suggest you may need to go back to the beginning and do the exercise again! But hopefully it has been a preparation for a deeper exploration of distinguishing between primary and secondary truth. In order to do this task, we have to ask: what is the core of evangelical belief?

Defining evangelical belief

For many years, the Bebbington quadrilateral has been a standard definition for defining evangelical belief.[11] The 'quadrilateral of priorities' according to David Bebbington are *conversionism*, the belief that lives need to be changed; *activism*, the expression of the gospel in effort; *biblicism*, a particular regard for the Bible and *crucicentrism*, a stress on the sacrifice of Christ on the cross. Mark Knoll calls this 'the most serviceable general definition' and Derek Tidball terms it 'as near to a consensus as we might reach'. To many, it has the advantage of being compact and quotable and, in Bebbington's judgment, these four priorities of the Bible, the cross, evangelism and conversion, are 'the common core of evangelicalism that has remained remarkably constant down the centuries'.[12]

There have been many attempts in recent years to refine the Bebbington definition.[13] I realise there is no simple formula but I appreciate the clarity which John Stott brings to the debate. He suggests the need to distinguish between divine and human activity (conversion and evangelism); between the primary and the secondary (the cross of Christ and the mode of baptism); between what belongs to the centre and what lies somewhere between the centre and the circumference (the authority of the Bible and the freedom of interpretation).

Stott proposes a Trinitarian formula for grounding historic evangelical identity, and suggests we are defined by the three 'R's of revelation, redemption and regeneration: we witness to the supreme authority of the word of God; we magnify the atoning sacrifice of Christ on the cross and we celebrate the life-giving ministries of the Holy Spirit. Holding firmly to these primary truths of the Bible, the cross of Christ and the Holy Spirit enables us to begin to distinguish between primary and secondary truth and it increases the potential for maintaining our gospel unity in the one faith for which we have to contend (Ephesians 4:5 and Jude 3).

I suggest three action points in the quest to distinguish between primary and secondary truth.

Confess the tendency to fragment

Firstly, we are prone to what John Stott terms 'our pathological tendency to fragment'.[14] It is the Achilles' heel of evangelicals that we divide so easily and so weaken the cause of evangelism in a local community.

I have visited most parts of the United Kingdom and it is heartbreaking to observe the ease with which new causes of evangelical work are started, with no reference to other evangelicals working in the same community. We seem to have imbibed a free market mentality for the church of Jesus Christ. There may be a 'Sainsburys' church – but we think what this town needs is a 'Morrisons' church. What does this attitude imply about relating to the body of Christ in the spirit of 1 Corinthians 12:21–26? Who challenges our tendency to fragmentation? What does this divisiveness do to the evangelistic witness of the church?

I believe our disunity deprives the world of an essential visual aid to believing in Jesus Christ (John 17:21). This chapter is a high-water mark of the fourth gospel as it summarises the message of the gospel and addresses the great themes of Jesus' obedience to his Father; the glorification of the Father through his death; the selection and the sending of the disciples in their mission; the unity of the disciples which is modelled on the unity of the Father and the Son, and the final destiny of the disciples in the glorious presence of the Father and the Son.

In the context of this glorious gospel summary, we have the prayer of Jesus for the unity of believers (17:21) which is unquestionably intended to be an observable unity but, as Don Carson says

> It is not achieved by hunting enthusiastically for the lowest common denominator, but by common adherence to the apostolic gospel, by love that is joyfully self sacrificing, by undaunted commitment to the shared goals of the mission with which the followers of Jesus have been charged, by self conscious dependence on God himself

for life and fruitfulness. It is a unity necessarily present
. . . amongst genuine believers; it is a unity that must be
brought to perfection.[15]

Make a commitment to meet together

The second step involves the leaders of all the evangelical tribes making a concerted commitment to meeting
together. I like the phrase of Don Carson – 'bringing our
unity to perfection', but for this to happen, national
evangelical leaders need to meet, pray and talk together
more than we are doing at present. I repeat what I have
previously suggested, that we need a summit conference
of evangelicals where our differences can be brought out
into the open. We need a forum where the core beliefs of
the evangelical tradition can be freely debated. This will
not be accomplished in one gathering; it is a process that
will take time, patience and understanding. It is within
an ongoing evangelical forum, where all the tribes are
represented, that we can begin to distinguish between
primary and secondary truth.

Cultivate a disposition of humility

The third action point is more personal and involves disposition. It is a call to self examination regarding our
attitude to other believers. It requires us to come before
the Lord and ask him to show us if we have any tenden-
cies to pride and prejudice. What is our 'world view' of
the evangelical scene and how does this influence the
way we relate to other believers?

   E.J. Poole-Connor was the founder of the Fellowship
of Independent Evangelical Churches and a doughty

contender for the evangelical faith. He held strong views
on not remaining in 'mixed' denominations with those
who denied evangelical principles. In spite of this
strength of conviction, one of the primary concerns and
longings of his life was for unity among evangelical
Christians, and in 1942 he set out the sum of his
thoughts in the book *Evangelical Unity*.

This book was an examination of the causes of division
and the evils of sectarianism and included a study on
revival and evangelical reunion. Poole-Connor observed
that, in times of revival, the Holy Spirit pays little attention to the party walls that we so carefully build up. He
believed that whatever our denominational affiliations,
all who profess Jesus Christ as the Head of the church are
blessed, because the Lord favours none and he refuses
none. Many volumes have been written by evangelical
Christians on the correct interpretation of Ephesians 4:5
where Paul speaks of the 'one faith' and predictably there
are many disagreements on how to define 'one'! But this
is what Poole-Connor says

> The utmost that anyone can say is that his creed is a
> statement of scriptural truth as he sees it and therefore
> binding on his conscience. To attempt to make it binding
> on that of his brethren, and to exclude them from com-
> munion because their interpretation of the 'one faith' is
> different from his, is to claim for an exegesis of Scripture
> the infallibility of Scripture itself.[16]

Distinguishing between primary and secondary truth is an
important step towards strengthening our unity. It requires
all three of these action points – confessing our pathological
tendency to fragment; leaders committing to meet together
to discuss core evangelical beliefs and all of us cultivating a
disposition of humility. From the seventeenth century,

evangelicals at their best have subscribed to the proverb which was made popular by Puritan Richard Baxter

Unity in essentials
Liberty in non-essentials
Charity in all things.

Questions

1. What is your view of the primary and secondary truths advanced in the chapter? Would you add or remove any of those views?
2. Read through the checklist of priorities expected of an evangelical church and decide which statements are a near reflection of your church. Is there another way of presenting your church to a watching world? If so, draw up a better description.
3. You are involved in a church plant and are at the stage of drawing up vision and mission statements. What 'belief' statements do you consider to be fundamental to an evangelical community, as viewed by not-yet Christians?

Books

I. Howard Marshall, *A Concise New Testament Theology* (Nottingham: IVP, 2009).

Bruce Milne, *Know the Truth* (Nottingham: IVP, 1998).

J.I. Packer, *Knowing God* new edition (London: Hodder, 2005).

John Stott, *Basic Christianity* (Nottingham: IVP, 2008).

Dave Tomlinson, *Re-enchanting Christianity: Faith in an Emerging Culture* (London: Canterbury Press, 2008).

Part three

Issues that divide

Chapter 6

Battles over the Bible

One of the ways we sustain evangelical unity is by a common fidelity to the authority of Scripture. In Kenneth Kantzer's memorable phrase, 'It is the Bible, the whole Bible and nothing but the Bible.' Evangelicals have a high view of Scripture and believe in the divine inspiration and supreme authority of the Old and New Testament Scriptures, which are the written word of God – fully trustworthy for faith and conduct.

Evangelicals are not unique in holding to the authority of the Bible, but what sets them apart as a distinct movement is the primary emphasis they place on this doctrine and the implications they draw from it. One of the sad paradoxes of the evangelical movement is that a doctrine which is given such primacy can also be the source of such dissension and brokenness. Most of our disagreements concern competing claims over what the Bible says about a particular doctrine. One example of how evangelicals engage in battles over the Bible concerns how we interpret the book of Revelation.

When Tim LaHaye and Jerry Jenkins published *Left behind: a novel of the Earth's Last Days* in 1995, I doubt if anyone envisaged that eleven titles later, total sales for the series would have surpassed 65 million copies and it would compete with John Grisham on the bestseller lists. It is easy to see why the *Left Behind* books are a publishing success in a world where religious extremism and terrorism go hand in hand, and millions of people are looking for answers to some of today's most pressing questions concerning the future. Will the conflict between Israel and Palestine escalate into a global nuclear conflict? Is God always on the side of Israel, whatever the nation does militarily? Has the 2009 meltdown of the financial world markets brought about the collapse of capitalism to match the 1989 collapse of communism? Are there Bible verses which predict this global crisis? Do these world events bring the return of Christ nearer? What should we do, as Christians, while we wait for the second coming? Do we seek to change the world? Is there any need for evangelism, if the coming of Jesus is very near? The appeal of the *Left Behind* books is to seemingly provide answers to anxious people concerned about such questions, and they offer readers the hope that God is at work in his world and the return of Christ is imminent.

Whilst evangelicals unite around one central truth concerning the last things and can affirm 'the personal and visible return of Jesus Christ to fulfil the purposes of God, who will raise all people to judgement, bring eternal life to the redeemed and eternal condemnation to the lost, and establish a new heaven and new earth' (Evangelical Alliance Basis of Faith revised edition 2005), there is a variety of interpretations on the last things and this diversity is headlined by Derek Tidball in a series of questions

- Will Jesus Christ return before or after the millennium or does it not matter? (The Millennium refers to

Revelation 20:2 and the thousand year reign of Satan: debate surrounds whether this is a figurative expression for the period between Christ's first and second coming or a literal period of time in the future.)
- Will the church be raptured? (This refers to 1 Thessalonians 4:13–17 when believers will be raptured or caught up in the air to meet Christ at his second coming.)
- Will Christ first come for his church and then come yet again to complete his work of judgment and recreation?
- Will the new creation be heaven or a new heaven and a new earth?
- And what about hell – will those who die without repenting be eternally punished or annihilated?
- And when will all this happen – tomorrow or later?[17]

Evangelical disunity is not only about what the Bible teaches about the second coming of Jesus Christ. Serious divisions have openly emerged in the past two decades over the nature of the atonement, homosexuality, women in pastoral ministry and Open Theism.[18]

The ancient words of the Westminster Confession are often cited as a concise summary for the core evangelical belief concerning the Bible: 'The whole counsel of God, concerning all things necessary for his glory, man's salvation, faith and life, is either expressly set down in Scripture, or by good and necessary consequence may be deduced from Scripture; to which nothing at any time may be added, whether by new revelations of the Spirit or traditions of men.'[19]

Our current debates raise the question about the final authority of the Scriptures in the life of the church. I believe it is important to restate some core beliefs concerning the Bible and state some ground rules for interpreting the Scriptures.

The Bible's witness to itself

In bearing witness to this fundamental principle, evangelicals first emphasise *the Bible's own teaching about itself* and the classic passage on inspiration with which to begin is 2 Timothy 3:16: 'All Scripture is God-breathed and is useful for teaching, rebuking, correcting and training in righteousness.'

I was brought up on the King James Authorised Version of the Bible, which says 'all Scripture is given by inspiration of God', but the NIV phrase 'God-breathed' is a more accurate translation of the Greek word. Just as God breathed into the body of Adam and he became a living being (Gen. 2:7), so God breathed his words into the writers of the Bible and they became his living words: collectively the word of God. God breathing his words and the human activity of writing are seen as complementary: 'But prophecy never had its origin in the will of man, but men spoke from God as they were carried along by the Holy Spirit' (2 Pet. 1:21).

'God-breathed' is a stronger word than 'inspiration' as it underlines the nature of the process by which the words of Scripture were produced. The word 'inspire' could mean a Bible writer was 'inspired' in the same way poets, musicians and artists are 'inspired' to write, compose and paint. Instead, Scripture affirms that God actually breathed his words into the personality, experience and gifts of various writers to produce his word.

This does not imply that the authors of Scripture were mechanics, nothing more than human typewriters who were in a trancelike state when writing: rather the totality of their humanity was operating during the writing process. God uses many different approaches

- The detective-style methods of Luke 'who carefully investigated everything from the beginning' (Luke 1:3) when he wrote the orderly account of his gospel.
- The fast-paced style of Mark, who bypasses the first thirty years of the life of Jesus and dives in at the beginning of his brief gospel with the ministry of John the Baptist and the baptism of Jesus.
- The poignant experiences of a brokenhearted husband, as Hosea shares his prophecy on God's grief for his unfaithful wife Israel.
- The gifted musicianship and poetry of the psalmists who had honed their words of praise in years of service in temple worship.
- The soaring logic and spiritual passion of Paul, as he climbs the 'Mount Everest' of Romans 8.
- The soul of a brokenhearted pastor, as Paul sits in a prison cell and writes his farewell words to his young friend (2 Tim. 4:9–18).

The ultimate part of the process of these 'God-breathed' words of the Bible is seen in their purpose of building up the church (2 Tim. 3:16–17). When the inspired word is preached, then the Scriptures are revealed in their life-changing power. They are useful for the wholesome teaching of the way of Christ; for the negative rebuttal of false teaching which detracts from the centrality of Christ; for the necessary correction of wrong behaviour for those who are disciples of Jesus Christ and for the positive training of believers in how to live a godly lifestyle in a godless world (2 Tim. 3:1–9). The end result is we are thoroughly equipped to serve God in his world. What a gift of grace!

Jesus' attitude to the Bible

Jesus so identified himself and his ministry with the Old
Testament Scriptures as to make the bond inseparable.
The Old Testament was the place where Jesus heard his
Father's voice. As you read the gospels, you learn that
Jesus attached the highest significance to the Old
Testament. The way he quotes the Scriptures reveals his
mind was saturated with God's words.

Jesus commenced his synagogue ministry in Nazareth
by preaching from Isaiah 61:1–2 and, when he had finished reading the scroll, he said: 'Today this Scripture
has been fulfilled in your hearing' (Luke 4:18–19). Jesus
was claiming he was the Messiah of whom Isaiah wrote
and the early church accepted this same interpretation of
the prophetic writings, as illustrated by Philip's
encounter with the African diplomat who had obtained
the words of Isaiah 53. When the African questioned the
meaning of the passage, Philip began with Isaiah 53,
'and told the man the good news about Jesus' (Acts
8:35). Philip must have learnt from the apostles this
Jesus method of reading and interpreting the Old
Testament, and this attitude to Scripture was basic to the
early preaching of the apostles as they bore witness to
Jesus as the fulfilment of the Old Testament. As Martin
Luther would say centuries later: 'the Scriptures are the
swaddling clothes and manger in which Jesus Christ is
laid.'

Jesus used the Scriptures when disputing with the
aristocratic Sadducees, who believed that resurrection
from the dead was a ludicrous concept. They attempted
to trick him with their question about a hypothetical
woman who became the bride for seven brothers. His
response was to tell them they were wrong because they
were ignorant of the Scriptures and the power of God

(Matt. 22:29). As religious leaders, the Sadducees knew the Scriptures. The problem was they had not penetrated into the meaning of the word which would have revealed to them the power of God to raise the dead. As Dick France says, it was a double error: 'a failure to understand Scripture which leads to an inability to appreciate what God can do.'[20]

The way Jesus used the Old Testament validates its authority as God's word which cannot be broken (John 10:35). Everything God had spoken through the prophets would be fulfilled (Luke 18:31–33). Jesus appealed to the authority of Scripture when he was tested by the Devil (Matt. 4:1–11). In reply to Satan's tempting suggestions, three times Jesus uses words from Deuteronomy to underline he is committed to living by God's word. For instance

- When Satan tempts him with food – Jesus says God's provision is sufficient for him (Deut. 8:3)
- When Satan tempts him with the spectacular – Jesus says God's way is best for him (Deut. 6:16)
- When Satan tempts him with power – Jesus says God alone has his loyalty (Deut. 6:13)

It is irrefutable that Jesus Christ himself saw Scripture as God-given.

The authority of the Bible over our lives

Because Scripture testifies to the God-breathed words of the Bible and Jesus affirmed the authority of God's word in his life and ministry, then we are to acknowledge the authority of the Bible over our lives as followers of Jesus. His allegiance to the authority of Scripture should be ours as well, which is why we believe that Christ rules his church through Scripture alone.

It is an evangelical distinctive to affirm *sola scriptura* (Scripture alone): as John Stott has memorably described, King Jesus rules his church with the sceptre of Scripture. This is not to deny the value of tradition and the use of human reasoning and experience but we do not place them in equal position alongside Scripture. If Scripture is the only source from which we gain our true knowledge of God, then the church sits humbly under the authority of this same Scripture.

So this is the implication. God the Holy Spirit was the agent who brought the biblical writings into being, as he breathed God's words through the writers; God the Holy Spirit anointed Jesus to be the Living Word in his life and ministry; and God the Holy Spirit now mediates the authority of Scripture in the church as he witnesses with our spirits to the truth of the Bible. In each generation, the authority of God's word comes to life through the ministry of the Holy Spirit.

I have encountered dozens of people who have commenced a spiritual journey to faith in Jesus, a journey sometimes lasting years, by first reading the Bible and then discovering that God's book was *the* great story where they found meaning to the lesser story of their lives. Jesus has assured us that when God's word is read in humble faith, then the Spirit of Truth bears clear witness to him (John 15:26).

The truthfulness of Scripture

It is in defining this that some of the fiercest conflicts have been fought over Scripture. Because the God of truth is the Author of Scripture, then the Bible is the book of truth. From beginning to end, the Bible is a revelation of the God of truth (Ps. 31:5; Is. 65:16; John 3:33); of Jesus as the embodiment of this divine truth (John 14:6; Eph. 4:21); and the Holy Spirit of truth who is our Guide (John 14:17 and 16:13). We are called to be a community of truth as we worship in spirit and truth (John 4:24) and teach spiritual truth in spiritual words (1 Cor. 2:13).

Evangelical statements support this truthfulness of Scripture by using words such as *reliable, infallible* and *inerrant*. By *reliable* and *infallible* we mean the Bible is totally trustworthy and true; by *inerrant* we mean the Bible is without error in every detail, not just in teaching on faith and practice, but also in the statements made on history, geography, astronomy and measurement.

Jim Packer explains the use of *infallible* and *inerrant* with this precise definition

> Infallible denotes the quality of never deceiving or misleading and so means wholly trustworthy and reliable; inerrant means wholly true. Scripture is termed infallible and inerrant to express the conviction that all its teaching is the utterance of the God who cannot lie. Once his word is spoken it abides for ever and therefore may be trusted implicitly. To assert biblical inerrancy and infallibility is to confess faith in (i) the divine origin of the Bible and (ii) the truthfulness and trustworthiness of God.[21]

In 1989 there was a Consultation on Evangelical Affirmations by nearly seven hundred evangelical scholars, theologians and leaders, which was co-sponsored by the National Association of Evangelicals and Trinity Evangelical Divinity School. Following the consultation the organisers published the papers in a book which assembles affirmations which are not intended to be a full confession of faith or a test of fellowship, but rather a confession of basically what it means to be evangelical. The signatories included Don Carson and Jim Packer and the statement on the Bible includes the following clauses

> We affirm the complete truthfulness and the full and final authority of the Old and New Testament Scriptures as the Word of God written. The appropriate response to it is humble assent and obedience . . . Evangelicals hold the Bible to be God's Word and, therefore, completely true and trustworthy (and this is what we mean by the words *infallible* and *inerrant*). It is the authority by which they seek to guide their thoughts and their lives.[22]

This basic evangelical affirmation should be a sufficient means to unite us around our commitment to the authority of Scripture in the life of the church. Any attempts to bolster our belief in the Bible by insisting on the use of particular words may result in an unnecessary and sinful division of the body of Christ.

In the current climate, I sense in our desire to defend the Bible evangelicals could be falling prey to the dangers of fundamentalism. Evangelicals differ basically from fundamentalists in their approach to the Bible. In fundamentalism, the Bible becomes an object to defend. The leading question of the fundamentalist is, 'What is your doctrine of Scripture?' In the evangelical tradition, the prime purpose of the Bible in the life of the church is to nurture God's people. The Scriptures are for our nourishment both in private study and public proclamation. We come to the Bible not to stand protectively over it but to sit under it humbly and to be fed with the Bread of Life.[23]

We next turn to a consideration of how we interpret the Bible and distinguish between the competing interpretations of Scripture among evangelicals.

Questions

1. Spend some time meditating on a Scripture passage of your choice and then ponder why this part of the Bible is so meaningful to you. Can 'meditation' give greater insight into the meaning of the text, or do we still need teachers and preachers to fully explain the passage?
2. Is it necessary to 'fall out' with other believers who have a different way of describing the authority of the Bible? Can we still enjoy close fellowship with others even if we have doctrinal differences? What is the minimum basis of fellowship?
3. What is good teaching and good preaching? Are there certain features present that you notice when the teacher/preacher appears to be inspired?

Books

D.A. Carson and John D. Woodbridge, *Scripture and Truth* (Grand Rapids: Baker, 1992).

J.I. Packer, *God has Spoken: Revelation and the Bible* (Grand Rapids MI; Baker, 1994).

N.T. Wright, *The Last Word: Beyond the Bible Wars to a New Understanding of the Authority of Scripture* (San Francisco: Harper, 2005).

Chapter 7

But the Bible says . . .

What does it take for a person to obey all the commandments of the Bible?

The Year of Living Biblically is a humorous and thought-provoking book by A.J. Jacobs which tells the story of his quest to live the ultimate biblical life. The author is a journalist from a secular Jewish background.

Jacobs decided to observe every single rule in the Bible as literally as possible. He began with the intention of examining the whole of the Bible but most of his book concerns his attempt to obey the Ten Commandments and the hundreds of oft-ignored commands. He refuses to mix wool with linen in his clothing; tries his hand at a ten-string harp; grows a beard; eats chocolate-covered crickets to fulfil Leviticus 11:22; pays the babysitter in cash at the end of each work day; offers practical advice on eating Ezekiel bread made of wheat, rye, millet, lentils and beans (which for the really committed is cooked over cow dung!): all to fulfil what Ezekiel did in Ezekiel 4:9.

He says his year of living biblically was fascinating, entertaining and informative. Jacobs explored some of the Bible's startlingly relevant rules: trying not to covet, gossip or lie for a year. As a journalist, he confesses this was not easy. He also investigated some of the teaching of the OT that baffled his 21st century brain: how do you justify the laws about stoning homosexuals? Or smashing idols? Or sacrificing oxen? And how do you follow these laws, living in modern-day New York?

Living for some time with various religious groups who take the Bible literally in their own way, he found himself with Samaritans in Israel, snake-handlers in Appalachia, Amish in Philadelphia and biblical creationists in Kentucky. By becoming an ultra-fundamentalist he became a critic of fundamentalism, finding that while fundamentalists may claim to take the Bible literally, actually they just pick and choose certain rules to follow. He found that interpreting the Bible literally just didn't work, for himself or anyone else, however motivated.

Jacobs says the year was a spiritual journey and confesses that, as an agnostic, he had never seriously explored such things as sacredness and revelation. His conclusion at the end of the year was that life was a choice between rights and responsibilities and the biblical way is to see life as engaging with responsibilities. He struggled with how to interpret the Bible and found its meaning frustratingly slippery. He realised his most significant spiritual experiences happened not when he was reading the Bible in a solitary place, but when he was enjoying the company of those who sought to obey the truths of the Bible in a religious community.

His most profound conclusion was the realisation that it is impossible to keep all these laws. However much he tried to observe the commandments of the Bible, he failed, and it was eye-opening to see the extent of his failure. In a deeply moving way, he suggests that he could not get a handle on the deeper message of the Bible and felt outmatched in trying to interpret its meaning.

A.J. Jacobs's experiences underline a basic truth on how to read the Bible. There is no point in having a Bible if you are not able to interpret it properly. So what are the ground rules for interpreting the Bible?

• Approach the Bible with humility

The Bible should be approached humbly, with the reminder that it is like no other book. This is God's book and these are God's words and, to interpret it correctly, we need God's help. Spiritual truths can only be understood with the help of the Holy Spirit, otherwise the words appear foolish to our natural understanding (1 Cor. 2:13–14). We must always breathe the prayer of the psalmist as we begin to read the Bible: 'Open my eyes that I may see wonderful things in your law' (Ps. 119:18).

• Many writers: one Author

The Bible was written by over forty writers over a period of fourteen hundred years but it has only one Author (2 Tim. 3:16; 2 Pet. 1:20–21): God the Holy Spirit. This single authorship means that when parts of the Bible seem to disagree, then we must search for Scriptures which speak more clearly. The rule is to let Scripture be its own interpreter. The command and accompanying promise of Exodus 20:24 ('Make an altar of earth for me and sacrifice on it your burnt offerings and fellowship offerings, your sheep and goats') do not mean 21st century Christians have to sacrifice sheep and goats. This passage must be read alongside passages which show the development of the sacrificial system, which culminates in the sacrifice of

Jesus Christ. John directs us to look at Jesus Christ as the sacrificial Lamb of God who takes away the sin of the world (John 1:29) and this is supported by Peter, who says our redemption is by the precious blood of Christ, a lamb without blemish or defect (1 Pet. 1:18–19).

• Christ is the focal point

The Bible is written to lead us to faith in Christ and all the Scriptures find their meaning in him. Always interpret the Bible with reference to Jesus Christ, for he gives the whole Bible its unity and meaning. When Jesus, after his resurrection, met the disciples on the road to Emmaus and confronted their sadness and confusion, he started at the beginning of the Bible with the books of Moses and went on through the prophets, pointing out everything in the Scriptures that referred to him (Luke 24:27). Luther was correct to observe 'Take Christ from the Scriptures and what more will you find in them?'

• What was their world?

The Bible has come to us through human writers who lived and wrote in a particular time and social context. As we have seen from studying 2 Timothy 3:15–17, God breathed his words to produce Holy Scripture but this divine inspiration was given in a specific context. When you start to read the book of Revelation, it is of fundamental importance to enter the world of the original writer. When and where did John write his vision? What can we discover about the social and political conditions in which he wrote? It makes all the difference to reading the book to discover that the author may have been an eighty-year-old pastor imprisoned on an island called Patmos. He was writing towards the latter part of the first century when the church had already experienced persecution from the Roman Emperor Nero and, in cities like John's home base of Ephesus, a climate of such fierce opposition was developing against Christians that it led many believers to feel they were living in the last days. It is also important to realise that the visions and symbols John employs in his book are not only a reflection of his immediate social context, but a timeless revelation of the cosmic struggle with the evil powers in every generation until the return of Christ in glory.

• Why did they write?

What was the writer's purpose? Look at the writing style. Is it an eye-witness account of an historical event? Is it poetry? Is it a parable with one punchline? Whatever the writing style, you are looking for the intentions of the author. Reading the Bible begins by seeking what has been termed the 'pastness of the past'. For example, what is Paul's purpose in retelling the complex episode in Abraham's life in Galatians 4, where he had fathered two sons? The spiritual interpretation of the passage is challenging but we are helped by Paul when he says he is speaking in figurative terms (Gal. 4:24). By employing an allegorical interpretation, Paul discerns a hidden spiritual meaning in the original text, a meaning that was unseen in the original passage in Genesis. Paul is not expounding the meaning as intended by the original writer. He is speaking of the meaning conveyed to him by a spiritual reading, in the light of the coming of Jesus and the unfolding story of the New Testament. Paul has discovered lasting spiritual truths buried in the tangled relationships of Abraham's family life.

• Context! Context! Context!

It is vital to remember that the context of a single verse of Scripture is the entire Scripture. Whatever passage is being studied, it must not only be seen in its immediate context but in harmony with the whole revelation of the Bible. One verse from Galatians 4 has first to be seen in the context of one book and then in the wider context of the library of 66 books.

I can remember the Keswick wall calendars in my home from my teenage years, which had a verse and comment for the day. My parents also had a promise box of Bible verses. With a pair of tweezers, you extracted from the box one of the tightly rolled pieces of paper on which was written a verse of Scripture, designed to bring hope and encouragement to the reader.

The equivalent in 2009 is the verse of the day which lands on your computer first thing in the morning. None of these aids to devotions are wrong in themselves but we need to heed the warning that the Bible must not be used as a personal scrapbook of favourite verses, chosen at random.

• What do others say?

It is important to listen to the wider community of believers when interpreting the Bible. The Bible is freely accessible to each believer but we are not meant to handle the Scriptures as our private possession. We may believe in the priesthood of all believers and the right to personal interpretation, but God has also given us the fellowship of the church in which we can share our insights of Scripture. We do not need the authority of a religious leader to have the final word on what the Scripture says; nor do we depend wholly on the technical expertise of Bible experts before arriving at a conclusion. This is our freedom but it is a sacred birthright that needs safeguarding. This is why God has gifted some to be Bible teachers and, through their gifting, the church is protected from error in teaching and built up in its holy faith. We expect our teachers to have a healthy respect for the biblical scholars who have devoted a lifetime to studying God's word. Their work is intended to assist the ministry of local teachers who interpret the Scriptures for us in a popular and understandable way. Good Bible teachers will introduce us to the rich insights which have emerged from teachers in the Christian community stretching back through two thousand years.

• The natural meaning

Read the Bible for its natural and obvious meaning. The parable of the Good Samaritan (Luke 10:25–37) can be misinterpreted with high levels of allegorical imagination where each part of the story symbolises an important part of truth.

One ancient interpretation of this parable suggests that the man who was travelling on the road symbolised Adam. Jerusalem was the paradise he had forfeited, and Jericho symbolises the world. The robbers are hostile to the Christian gospel; the priest stands for the Law; the Levite is a symbol of the prophets and the Samaritan is Christ. The wounds inflicted on the traveller are disobedience; the donkey which carries the wounded man is the Lord's body; the oil and the wine symbolise the Lord's Supper and the inn is the church. The manager of the inn symbolises those who lead the church, to whom its care has been entrusted. And the fact that the Samaritan promises he will return represents the Saviour's second coming!

This is very imaginative but not the natural and obvious meaning of the parable.

If we employ the rules of interpretation we will first look at the context for the story, which is a conversation between Jesus and a lawyer (Luke 10:25–29). The lawyer has posed two questions to Jesus: 'What must I do to obtain eternal life?' and 'Who is my neighbour?' In answer to the latter question, Jesus tells the parable (Luke 10:30–35). Finally, Jesus asks the lawyer who of the three men had been a neighbour to the man. Having received the correct answer, Jesus commands him to go and imitate the Good Samaritan's actions (Luke 10:36–37).

The wider context of the story will take into account the main theme which Luke has been expanding throughout his gospel, namely that God's grace and love through Jesus is for the least and the lost and those considered by religious people to be beyond the pale (Luke 7:31–35; Luke 19:1–10).

A natural and obvious reading of the parable is to understand the extreme cost involved in being the kind of neighbour God intends. The Good Samaritan was willing to overcome the barriers of prejudice; delay his travel plans; expose himself to danger; share his wealth and promise more money if needed; and finally commit himself to keep in touch with the victim. Can we, as we share the love of Christ, match this kind of costly commitment?

• Beware your culture

Remember to lay aside any cultural presuppositions when approaching the text. This rule is probably one of the most important to recognise for understanding the major debates we experience today. All of us bring cultural presuppositions to the Bible. We are shaped by our family backgrounds, how we live within the culture of a society, the church to which we belong, the conferences we attend, the books we read and the sermons we download from our favourite web sites. John Stott suggests that the first step toward recovering our Christian integrity is the

> humble recognition that our culture blinds, deafens and dopes us. We neither see what we ought to see in Scripture, not hear God's Word as we should, nor feel the anger of God against evil. We need to allow God's Word to confront us, disturbing our security, undermining our complacency, penetrating our patterns of thought and behaviour, and overthrowing our resistance.[24]

In the period before the American Civil War, Christians in the US were engaged in fierce debates over the rights and wrongs of slavery, and both sides drew on the Bible to support their views. Both groups believed in the authority of Scripture but were deeply divided over how to interpret it on this issue. There were those who supported slavery and believed the Bible endorsed the practice. Others believed it was an intrinsically evil institution and campaigned ceaselessly for its abolition. Both groups believed in the authority of the Bible but interpreted the Scriptures in radically different ways.

The main argument of the pro-slavery group was that the Bible nowhere condemns slavery. The practice of slavery is present throughout the period of the Old Testament. There are Scriptures on how owners are to treat their slaves, but nothing on abolition. A reading of the New Testament comes to similar conclusions. Again, an owner is taught how to treat their slaves (Eph. 6:5–9) but nowhere is the practice condemned.

Carl Sanders identifies the strategies of those who wanted to see slavery abolished. Firstly, they distanced modern slavery from the institution of slavery in the Bible and argued that the differences of the social contexts were so radical as to render the biblical slavery texts irrelevant to modern practice. They argued that any form of slavery that deprived people of their fundamental rights of liberty was prohibited in the Bible.

They also drew on broader theological principles. The creation story describes humans created in the image of God and made to rule over the earth. Slavery robs people of this God-given dominion and is therefore incompatible with God's intentions. Sanders concludes 'When combined with powerful cultural assumptions about race, most American evangelicals were unable to find resources to address the slavery questions effectively.'[25]

This debate over slavery underlines the difficulty of simply applying the letter of Scripture without taking wider biblical issues into account. It comes to the very heart of what lies behind our evangelical disunity over the interpretation of the Bible. How do we distinguish between those who have competing biblical interpretations on issues such as the ministry of ordained women and the nature and practice of human sexuality? How much are we faced (as with slavery) with a cultural context in the Bible which is totally different to our own and therefore should allow for cultural conditioning when interpreting the Bible for today? If the Bible says a woman should be silent in church, is this a permanent prohibition? Is the Bible text which commands stoning as the penalty for adultery so culturally conditioned it cannot be binding on us today?

• Facing critical areas of disagreement

John Stott is immensely helpful in the guidance he offers, first offering options for interpreting difficult Bible passages clothed in the culture of their day, and then outlining broader principles for facing critical areas of disagreement.[26]

Stott's options are:

1. *Total rejection.* We can say this is culturally irrelevant teaching and choose to ignore it.
2. *Wooden literalism.* We can say as this is part of God's word, it must be literally preserved and followed.
3. *Cultural transposition.* We can identify the essential thing God is saying here, separate it from the cultural form in which it is given, and then reclothe it in appropriate modern cultural terms in harmony with the rest of Scripture.

Total rejection is the position adopted by William M. Kent, a member of the committee assigned by USA United Methodists to study homosexuality. He declared that 'the scriptural texts in the Old and New Testaments condemning homosexual practice are neither inspired by God nor otherwise of enduring Christian value. Considered in the light of the best biblical, theological, scientific, and social knowledge, the biblical condemnation of homosexual practice is better understood as representing time and place bound cultural prejudice.'[27]

This option of total rejection of Bible verses cannot be considered seriously if we claim to be under the authority of God's word. We have to find other ways of interpreting the difficult passages of Scripture. We cannot just pick and choose those bits of Scriptures we agree with and say that these have authority.

Wooden literalism fails to distinguish between 'literalism and letterism' and leads to crude results. To impose the levitical laws on modern day believers is to wrench a prohibition out of its original context, which was Israel as an ancient nation administering social laws for its citizens. Many of the levitical commands are ignored by evangelicals on the grounds that we are not a civil nation administering justice. The punishments described are not appropriate for the church of Jesus Christ, which is why we do not condone stoning people for committing adultery or disobeying their parents. This caveat on ignoring letterism does not mean we can set to one side the spirit of the truth expressed in the biblical passages. The church will note those commands which have abiding significance for the people of God and, where there is conduct unbecoming by its members, will apply appropriate church discipline (See chapter 11).

Cultural transposition allows us to search for the truth in the text by looking for a wider interpretation in the whole of Scripture.

One of the most controversial areas of biblical interpretation which has exercised evangelicals is the ministry of women. Studying it shows the values of applying careful principles of interpretation to difficult Scripture passages, even when there may be different conclusions.

Women in leadership

The question of women in leadership ministry in the church continues to divide Christians. There is firm agreement that men and women are equal before God in creation and redemption. Together we bear God's image (Gen. 1:27) and share equally in the fruits of salvation in Christ (Gal. 3:26–28). The difficulties arise over passages which explicitly command women to be silent (1 Cor. 14:34–35) and to refrain from teaching or having authority over men (1 Tim. 2:11–12). Further passages point to the 'principle of headship' where the head of every man is Christ but the head of the woman is man (1 Cor. 11:3).[28]

Those in support of ordained women's ministry apply the principle of clarifying the meaning in these biblical texts and looking for a wider interpretation in the rest of Scripture. In particular they note:

- Most of the biblical references using the term headship are in the context of the marriage relationship
- In the two passages in context of church life (1 Cor. 11:2–16; 1 Tim. 2:9–15), it is not clear whether Paul is speaking of a woman's silence and submission to her husband or men in general
- Some say the 'principle of headship' permits a woman to minister under the responsibility of a male leader. Others say the term is ambiguous
- It is suggested that the one clear passage in 1 Timothy 2:11–12 relates to a unique local situation and should be read alongside the verses on widows in a parallel passage in 1 Timothy 5:11–15

These issues are explored more fully in the substantive literature on the subject.[29] Both sides of the debate can claim to have Scripture on their side. Those who restrict the role of women in ministry point to the prohibition texts and the principle of male headship. Those who celebrate the ministry of women say that Paul's comment 'there is no longer male or female' extends to ministry and his reference to female submission is restricted to marriage.

Pastoral attitudes

This issue has not only divided evangelicals in the way they interpret the Bible but the pastoral fall-out has been immense. Our attitudes have sometimes lacked grace and the tone of our debate has often not honoured Christ. Living under the authority of the Bible is not easy and the pastoral implications of obedience to Scripture needs to be alongside some wise pastoral guidelines. There is no place for misogyny in the church. You can be firm in your doctrinal views on the role of women in the church and still honour the gifts and calling of ordained women.

Questions

1. The Bible confirms that God creates and loves diversity. In your opinion, does this mean that such 'diversity' allows evangelical believers to stick to their 'tribal' communities?
2. Why is it that some evangelical Christians have become intolerant and arrogant towards other evangelical Christians who do not tick all the right theological boxes, in their view? Do you think it is possible for such believers and communities to change? How can we strike a right balance with such people?
3. Discuss with a friend how talking and listening can be used to improve relationships

- in a local church
- in a local cluster
- between different networks

Books

James R. Beck and Craig L. Blomberg, *Two Views on Women in Ministry* (Grand Rapids, Illinois: Zondervan, 2001).

R.T. France, *A Slippery Slope: A Case Study in Biblical Interpretation* (Cambridge: Grove Books, 2000).

Ronald W. Pierce and Rebecca Merrill Groothuis (eds.), *Discovering Biblical Equality: Complementarity Without Hierarchy* (Leicester: IVP, 2004).

John Piper and Wayne Gruden (eds.), *Recovering Biblical Manhood and Womanhood: A Response to Evangelical Feminism* (Wheaton Illinois: Crossway, 1991).

Sarah Sumner, *Men and Women in the Church: Building Consensus on Christian Leadership* (Downers Grove Illinois: InterVarsity, 2003).

Part four

Dangers to avoid

Chapter 8

Insights from a housegroup

There are dangers to avoid when relating to other believers. Is it possible to disagree with another believer without being disagreeable? What does it mean to relate to someone within what is called reconciled diversity? (This is the recognition that there can be genuine disagreements which remain unresolved.) Can we base our fellowship on the understanding that we will be reconciled while remaining in diversity? This chapter is a collection of insights from an imaginary housegroup which are intended to prepare the way for the biblical principles from Romans 14 and 15 in the following chapter.

It was the vicar's idea that St. Paul's should join the local churches' Lenten project and he asked Rob and Celia if their home could be a venue for one of the proposed housegroups.

There were two organisations in Broadham which gathered the churches for fellowship and joint action. Churches Together in Broadham (CTB) included most of the 22 churches of Broadham and the surrounding villages. Broadham Evangelical Fellowship (BEF) was a smaller grouping of twelve churches which included

some who were in CTB and other churches that in conscience could not belong to CTB, because of its 'mixed'
membership of Roman Catholics and churches which
did not claim to be evangelical.

Some of the church leaders in both CTB and BEF had
been meeting occasionally for coffee and fellowship
and had shared their mutual concerns about the spiritual and social needs of Broadham. Whilst there was no
desire to amalgamate the two bodies, they did want to
give a visual expression to the town of the core unity in
Christ that many had experienced, through their
friendships with believers from other Christian traditions.

So the leaders agreed to encourage their churches to
get involved in the six week Lenten project, beginning
on Ash Wednesday, which would culminate in an open-
air gathering on Good Friday in the town centre.

Rob and Celia were experienced leaders and had led
housegroups at St. Paul's for five years, but this was the
first time they had encountered a housegroup membership drawn from all the churches. Nine people arrived at
their house on the first evening. It was a good cross section of people representing different church backgrounds and the cultural diversity of Broadham, as well
as a good spread of ages and Christian experience.

After three weeks of the Lenten meetings, Rob and
Celia were invited to meet with their vicar, Stephen, for
a progress report and to share any difficulties they had
encountered. Attendance had been very consistent over
the first three weeks of the Bible studies and, apart from
a couple of tense moments, overall the group had begun
to gel. Prior to their meeting with the vicar, Rob and
Celia had drawn up a brief profile of each member of the
housegroup, and this was the first thing they shared
with Stephen.

Housegroup members

- Trevor and Grace were in their seventies and lifelong members of the local Methodist church. They were a pastoral couple and had been the first to learn the names of all the members of the group. They had lived in Broadham for over fifty years, had a good understanding of all the Christian traditions in the town and seemed to have friends and relatives in all of them. Trevor did not like the disagreements in the housegroup, which on a couple of occasions had become very contentious, and Rob and Celia had found it hard to get the group back on track. Trevor's response on both occasions was to suggest immediately they close in prayer and adjourn for tea and coffee.

- Andy and Shirley were in their early forties and were members of the Brethren chapel. They ran a wholesale fruit and vegetable company and were probably the earliest risers in the group, as their lorries were on route to Covent Garden in the early hours of each day. They both came from non-Christian homes and had been converted to Christ through a Christian mission at their agricultural college, and they shared an enthusiastic passion to see the whole of Broadham won to Christ. They felt the doctrinal differences which separated the churches were a scandal and repeatedly said in the housegroup 'Doctrine divides but evangelism unites.' This view brought them into direct conflict with Peter . . .

- Peter was an elder in the Baptist church and had studied theology through an online computer course with a reformed theological seminary in the USA. He was the most informed member of the housegroup when it came to Bible knowledge and, in his view, doctrine was of fundamental importance to the life and health of the church of Jesus Christ. To him, Andy and Shirley were naïve to cite the mantra, 'Doctrine divides but evangelism unites.' He thought that the church had sold out to secular methods of 'seeker sensitive' evangelism and had turned from a dependence on the all-sufficiency of God to a management-driven model of church life. He believed the current confusion in church over homosexuality was due to senior church leaders abandoning their belief in the final authority of Scripture. So, until he saw visible signs in all the churches in Broadham of a return to scriptural values, he would oppose any move for a united project in evangelism. He adroitly changed Andy and Shirley's favourite phrase into, 'When we are united in doctrine then we can be united in evangelism.'

- Peter's views, and how he expressed them in the housegroup, were challenged consistently by Liz, an orthopaedic surgeon and part of the leadership team in the Community church. Liz was calm and clinical in her contributions to the housegroup and, as Rob described it, you could sense the knife going in as she carefully dissected the issues which were under discussion and then sensitively challenged the views of other members. Liz was part of the speakers' team at the Community church and her sermons were widely appreciated. She knew Peter's negative views on the ministry of women and attempted to reason with him on some of the contentious passages of Scripture on the relationship between men and women and the role of women in church leadership. She concluded they had different rules for interpreting the Bible.

- Stefan was a bricklayer from Manchester whose parents were Polish Catholics. Although he had been baptised as a Catholic and attended Catholic schools until the age of seventeen, he had drifted from his cradle faith. His foreman on the building site was a member of the Salvation Army and, when he discovered Stefan was a trumpet player, invited him to play with the local band for the annual Christmas Carols in the shopping precinct. Gradually Stefan was drawn into the life of the local Salvation Army citadel and he had recently come to personal faith in Christ. He loved being in the Lenten housegroup. He found it immensely stimulating to discover that stories about Jesus that he had been taught at the Catholic school were now coming to life. Privately, he offered a prayer of thanks for the grounding in the Bible he had been given at school and wished he had the courage to express the conviction that God had always been working in his life from his earliest days. He feared, however, that some group members would not understand.

- Mary also felt unable to share her greatest concerns with the group. She was a member of Broadham Evangelical church which she had attended for forty years. It was in the same church's youth club that she had met Terry, whom she eventually married, and they had had two children. She was only 28 when Terry was diagnosed with cancer. Within months, he had died and she was left to bring up two young children alone. These children were now young adults who had left home, and her son Clive was a gifted primary school teacher working in a school in a deprived part of Leeds. It was a letter from her son that was causing her pain. He had written to say he had fallen in love with an architect called Ben and they were planning to live together. Clive was writing to ask if he could bring Ben to meet Mary over the Easter weekend.

Mary was desperate to share this news with some-one and she was in torment as to what to do. She felt reluctant to share with the group and Peter's openly expressed views, which were decidedly homophobic, were deepening her concerns.

- Essien was a student from Ghana studying econom-ics. He came from an African Pentecostal tradition and had found it a struggle to settle into any of the churches in Broadham. So, once a month, he travelled to East London to worship with a mainly Ghanaian congregation. He found that however friendly the local churches were, their welcome did not have the same warmth and informality as his home church in Kumasi, and his biggest complaint was the lack of earnest prevailing prayer. He was used to the whole church being involved in prayer times, so when the pastor prayed for the healing of a sick person, there would be loud shouts of prayer from all parts of the congregation. He liked services where people gave their testimonies verifying that God had healed them. Essien struggled with the housegroup debates on when to do evangelism, as to him sharing his faith in Jesus was as natural as breathing. He said, 'You breathe in the love of God in the morning and then breathe it out during the rest of the day!'

'So there you have our housegroup', Celia said to the vicar. 'You could not wish for a greater diversity of Christians.' 'We don't mind them discussing and debat-ing', said Rob. 'The question is, how do we get them to handle their diversity?' 'There is nothing new about that question', said Stephen. 'It was a question faced by those who were leaders two thousand years ago.' He then suggested that Rob and Celia study the letter to Romans, chapters 14–15 in particular, where Paul tack-les the issue of diversity in a local congregation.

They prayed together for the continued success of their housegroup and promised to update their vicar on the final three Bible study sessions.

Questions

1. Explain the tensions that exist between Peter and Liz and offer ways that could possibly resolve the situation. Find appropriate biblical material that could support a 'spirit of fellowship' to develop between the two of them.
2. The personal trauma facing Mary is a difficult pastoral matter. What advice would you give to Mary, and can situations like this be resolved without pain? How does this pastoral issue relate to unity in the local church when there are different views on homosexuality?
3 .Rob and Celia's housegroup is very diverse due mainly to the different churches represented in their home. What are the pluses and minuses to having cross-church discussions on questions such as unity between believers?

Books

Rob Frost, *Doing the Right Thing: Ten Issues on Which Christians Have to Take a Stand* (Oxford: Monarch, 2008).

Simon Jones, *Building a Better Body: The Good Church Guide* (Milton Keynes: Authentic, 2007).

Pete Ward, *Participation and Mediation: A Practical Theology for the Liquid Church* (London: SCM, 2008).

Chapter 9

Disagreeing without being disagreeable

Someone has suggested that the favourite sport of Christians is 'trying to change each other.' As Martin Luther said, every man naturally has a pope inside him. This is not to fudge on major issues, for sometimes there has to be a real separation from those who have clearly departed from an orthodox Christian faith. But we need to acknowledge that a real tension exists when Christians interpret the Bible in different ways. Our debatable areas of faith and conduct are based on our individual insights into Scripture, and then we act in these areas according to conscience. But what if my conscience approves what your conscience condemns? How can we stay together in fellowship, keeping the royal law of love? How are we to handle the inevitable friction of being in the same fellowship as another believer who does not see things as we see them? How can we disagree without being disagreeable?

Almost all churches can provide examples of such tensions. For example:

- A leaders' day conference is scheduled to take place at a country hotel which has a bad reputation for rowdy weekend stag parties. There have been press reports of drunken behaviour and violent assaults, and two of the church leaders think it is inappropriate to patronise this particular hotel because of its reputation for encouraging a drinking culture. The pastor had begun to build a relationship with the managers of the hotel and felt the leaders' conference could build further on this developing friendship and, in the long term, this could be a force for good in the community. The two opposing leaders are very concerned about the drinking habits of some of the young people in the church and suggest this is the moment for the church to take a moral stand. They threaten to pull out of the day conference unless the venue is changed.

• For many years, a city centre church near to a shopping mall has had some modest decorations outside the church during the Christmas season. Two new families join the church and suggest plans for brightening up the outside of the church to match the attractive Christmas decorations of the mall. The deacons give permission for the project without seeing the detailed plans. Both families have business links with marketing and design companies and acquire a giant Santa figure on a sledge which dominates the square in front of the church. Their idea is to play carols on Saturdays in December, serve hot punch and roasted chestnuts and give copies of a Jeff Lucas Christmas tract to shoppers. On the first Saturday, some members see the display and are appalled at the secular image it portrays. They request an emergency church meeting following the Sunday morning service. The two young families, supported by many church members, have been thrilled by the response they have received from passing shoppers. They anticipate their church could break attendance records for the annual carol service.

- As part of their centenary celebrations, a church is arranging a meal for 160 people in the local restaurant. The plans were approved months ago by the whole fellowship and it was agreed that the tickets would be on sale at £30. The restaurant has been booked and a deposit paid. With three weeks to go, thirty members have now decided it is an expensive luxury in the current financial climate and that it will bring unnecessary hardship. They are proposing a more modest supper to be held on church premises and are prepared to forfeit the deposit money. The church leadership believe it is right to honour this milestone anniversary in a special way and have suggested ways to ensure those who can't afford the ticket price can be included without any loss of dignity. They are also aware that the restaurant is going through a lean time and the owners are banking on the custom of the church.

Some wise decisions are called for in each of these situations and there are guidelines in Romans 14 and 15 which draw out some theological truths we can use for settling potentially divisive issues. I realise we are attempting to apply basic principles to a range of conflicting issues and I know that one person's secondary matter is another person's prime concern. I believe there are heretical views concerning the person and work of Jesus Christ which are not being addressed by the principles Paul outlines in Romans 14–15 (see later references on church discipline in chapter 14). These guidelines are for tackling the breakdown in relationships between those who hold equally valid views. In every community where there is conflict these guidelines need to be heeded. It is possible that neither side is totally in the right.

The church at Rome

It is worth remembering that Paul, without having visited Rome, is aware of the existence of at least two major groups in the church there, known as the 'weak' and the 'strong'. The 'weak' have tender consciences about matters of truth and lifestyle choices; the 'strong' are encouraged to recognise this and invited to forgo their right to exercise their freedom in Christ.

The 'weak' were probably vegetarians and total abstainers. Taking into account the similar situation outlined in 1 Corinthians 8–10, they may have objected to buying cut price meat from a market stall which they knew was sold cheaply because it had been obtained as leftovers from pagan temple sacrifices.

The 'weak' also had convictions about maintaining the Sabbath celebration as Saturday. Jewish believers felt strongly that observance of Saturday as the holy day was particularly pleasing to God, as it maintained links with the Jewish faith which had been the cradle into which Jesus had been born. Gentile Christians, however, with no Jewish background, had no wish to adopt a custom that was inconvenient as well as ridiculous in the eyes of Roman society.

The 'weak' were censorious towards those who did not share their convictions. They considered the 'strong' group both careless and indifferent and were convinced that someone had to maintain standards. The 'strong' said every day of the week belonged to God, so why make one day special? They said food was food, wherever it had been purchased and besides if you could save money by buying meat cheaply, you had more money to donate to the poor. The 'strong' enjoyed the freedoms of the gospel and despised those who hadn't entered the world of Christian liberty.

This is a familiar situation which resonates with church life today. One tribe considers the other lax; the other tribe considers their friends rigid. In such situations, Paul suggests, the over-riding criterion has to be: we must not only be true to our principles, but also consider the effect of our action on others. It is easy to identify modern day equivalents in the attitudes of these two groups of the 'weak' and the 'strong'. The 'strong' are usually in the majority. They consider the others stick-in-the-mud and traditional. They adopt that well-known attitude of group behaviour: 'As you are small in number you are not worth taking seriously.' The 'weak' are normally the minority. They consider that their colleagues have no scruples in matters of faith and that they take dangerous liberties with Scripture. They adopt an attitude of contempt and spiritual pride: 'Thank the Lord that *some* of us are faithful to the gospel.'

It has been a privilege, over the past few years, to share in the leadership of national workshops and seminars for pastors and church workers. The following question is typical of the questions which arise in a seminar group:

> We are an evangelical church which has been presented with an exciting mission vision by our leadership team. If we are serious about serving the spiritual and social needs of our community, this will involve a radical realignment of church life and a major redesign of our church premises. We have a congregation of 250 members, with a 'keen core' comprising over 60 per cent of regular attendees. There is a small but influential group who has been in the church for many years, who are saying we need to stick with traditional values of Bible teaching and evangelism. They consider our growing community involvement a 'slippery slope' which will

lead us away from the pure gospel. They say that any changes to the building will be 'over our dead bodies'. Can you offer suggestions on how to keep the church together? How can we bridge the growing gulf between the conservative element and those who want to move on with this vision? How can we motivate others in our church to share our God-given vision for missionary outreach to our needy community?

There is no easy answer to this scenario and a vision for a radical re-imagining of a church often takes longer to work through than we estimate. In my experience, there are two fundamental principles which enable a church family to survive such storms. The first is every church needs to open an investment account into which each member is encouraged to pay daily deposits of love, trust, goodwill and kindness. Then, in days of church crisis, we have something to draw upon. The second principle is that whatever labels my fellow-travellers wear, God has accepted them and therefore I dare not exclude them.

The particular issues of food, drink and holy days may not seem as relevant today, but the value of this passage lies in the permanent guidelines given to believers on how to disagree without being disagreeable. The first thing Paul says is there are attitudes we must avoid (Rom. 14:1–12).

• Do not exclude people when God has accepted them (verses 1–3)

Whenever there is a serious dispute with another believer, I must remember that this person also belongs to Jesus Christ and I must treat them as a brother or sister

in Christ. 'Welcome' and 'acceptance' are the key words
in these opening verses and, whatever our tribal allegiance, we are called to unreservedly recognise each
other. If God has accepted us into his family on the basis
of our trusting Jesus Christ, then we must not pass
judgment on one another.

When we practise this principle of acceptance, we are
acknowledging that the grace of God is at work in our
lives and he has the power to change people, beginning
with me!

In my heart, I may consider another believer bigoted
in their attitudes; lacking a heart for mission; over-
defensive about the purity of the church; having more
concern for historic buildings than for what God is
doing today. I must always begin by extending the hand
of friendship and accepting them as a genuine member
of the family.

• Do not interfere in the life of another disciple: God is in charge (verse 4)

When we disagree with other believers, there is the
temptation to play the role of God in their lives. This
verse reminds us that believers enjoy a master-servant
relationship with the Lord and this must never be
interfered with: 'Who are you to judge someone else's
servant? To his own master he stands or falls. And he
will stand, for the Lord is able to make him stand'
(14:4).

For many years, it was my privilege to lead housegroups for new Christians, and in this setting I always
had to be on my guard when I discovered people did not
share my personal convictions. As a Bible teacher, I do
have the responsibility to teach the word of God to

young believers and 'correct, rebuke and encourage with great and careful instruction' (2 Tim. 4:2). The essentials of truth and doctrine must be taught and grasped and there is a proper place for saying with Paul 'I urge you to imitate me' (1 Cor. 4:16). But I need to remember my prime task is to make disciples of Jesus. It is the work of the Holy Spirit firstly to convict of truth and then to influence the shaping of these truths in areas of personal belief and behaviour. His work of enlightening will not necessarily be immediate, and he may choose different methods to bring people to a point of renewal of mind and conduct.

I have views on Sabbath observance. So, when a Sunday cricket league player was converted and joined our church, he asked if it was all right for him to continue to play on Sunday. I could offer him some guidelines based on the Bible, but I could not make the decision for him.

I have strong views on the political bias of sections of the media and am a champion for a truly independent press. When a journalist was converted through the Alpha programme and told me which newspaper he worked for (I did not flinch!), I initiated a conversation with him on the biblical values of truth and decency in the media, and left him to consider whether he thought it was right for him to continue writing for this particular journal.

I have to resist taking these decisions for my friends. I can teach the Scriptures and outline the pattern of sound doctrine. I can pray and advise but, when God is in charge of a person's life, I must not interfere in the relationship. So why do we break this golden rule? Because the spiritual welfare of our friend is our highest concern and we want the very best for them? But this verse reminds us that the primary responsibility for the spiritual welfare of our friends belongs to the Lord. As the verse says, to their own master they stand or fall.

I do have a major responsibility as a pastor/teacher. But the Lord is more concerned about the development of a disciple than we could ever be. Because it suits his purposes to see a disciple maturing, the Lord will have his ways of training them in his work.

• Do not base your views on prejudice: remember God is Lord of the mind (verses 5–10)

Most of us know what it is like to be under pressure to conform. I have seen how people make decisions in meetings where voting is by a show of hands. Some folk are a split second late in putting their hands up, as they need to see which way influential members are casting their vote. When we are confronted with conflicting convictions, here is a further principle to adopt: 'Each one should be fully convinced in his own mind' (14:5). Note the number of times the title 'Lord' is used in verses 5–10, indicating that we are expected to form our convictions in Christ. Our minds are being renewed by the regular teaching of the gospel (Rom. 12:2). We should use our individual powers of reasoning to form our own judgments as to what specific obedience the gospel requires.

This is not to deny the role the church community may play in offering discernment and guidance to the individual. But what these verses are commanding is that we must never adopt a pattern of behaviour *merely* because others teach and practise it. The will of the Lord for my life is paramount. Jesus had to remind Peter of this when he showed undue curiosity over the Lord's plans for his friend John (John 21:22).

• Do not condemn – remember God is the judge (verses 10–12)

Paul uses here the family term *adelphos* – brother. The other believer, brother or sister, with whom you disagree, is in the fullest sense a member of God's family: 'You then, why do you judge your brother? Or why do you look down on your brother?' It is patently clear that this freedom of the individual has parameters. If a Christian home becomes a place of physical violence or sexual abuse, the Christian community is bound to intervene and support the legal process of bringing wrongdoers to justice. If a business run by a Christian, who is also an elder in his local church, mistreats its employees, fails to pay its bills and has a reputation for shoddy work, then the local church has a duty to confront the elder. This may lead to a process of temporary discipline. But in matters of private conviction, where no harm is being done to either the community or another believer, then the Lord alone has the right to judge how we live our lives. Each of us will give an account of our stewardship to him (v12). We should not anticipate that occasion of which Paul speaks elsewhere: 'Therefore judge nothing before the appointed time; wait until the Lord comes. He will bring to light what is hidden in darkness and will expose the motive of men's hearts' (1 Cor. 4.5).

Having dealt with attitudes we must avoid, if we are going to disagree without being disagreeable, Paul turns next to consider the dispositions we need to cultivate in relating to other believers (Rom. 14:13–23).

It might seem that Paul has been suggesting, 'Let sleeping dogs lie; let's ignore our differences and pretend they don't exist.' However, his appeal is not to moral generalities like broadmindedness and tolerance, but to the very heart of what God has done and has given us in Jesus Christ. It is because his principles are so theological that his touch is so unerring. As we mentioned in the last section, we must recognise that individual freedom of conscience has its limits. We must take into account the effect our actions may have upon others.

• Seek to be a good influence (verses 13–15)

The emphasis is now turned towards the impact our behaviour may have on other people. Paul reflects the teaching of Jesus, when he said to his disciples, 'Things that cause people to sin are bound to come, but woe to that person through whom they come' (Luke 17:1).

We need to reflect on the compelling words that Paul employs in these verses. He is talking about not putting a stumbling block in your brother's path: distressing your brother by what you do and destroying your brother by your actions. Paul reminds us that we have the power to contribute to the spiritual ruin of another person by insisting on outwardly exercising our freedoms. By thoughtlessly behaving in this way, we can stand accused of no longer acting in love. Our love for another believer should always be the principal motive in situations of strife.

I find Jim Packer's illustration of the football referee helpful in this connection.[30] Football referees do four things: they are familiar with the rules and their interpretation; they position themselves in the best place on the field; they can consult impartial linesmen but ignore partisan crowds; and they can play the 'advantage rule' if it benefits the wronged side.

Our loving consideration for another believer is similar. It requires us to know the Scriptures without which good decisions are impossible; we need to be in the best position for decision-making, secure as much information as we can on causes and consequences; we can consult those who may be better qualified and, at the same time, decline to be swayed by the ill-informed. Finally, we can apply the advantage rule by not jeopardising a greater good by needless inquiry (see Romans 14:14–16).

Christians live by the forgiveness of sins, so they need not be afraid to fail and in humility learn from their mistakes. Just as referees can make bad decisions, so Christians may miss the best course of action and make errors of judgment. 'If your brother is distressed . . . you are no longer acting in love' (v15).

• Seek to establish priorities (verses 16–18)

I can imagine someone protesting to Paul, 'But what about my freedom? Why should my liberty be challenged by someone who is frustratingly petty?' To return to our earlier examples, does this mean agreeing with the two leaders who have a conscience over the hotel with a reputation for drunken behaviour? Dismantling the Santa feature outside the church? Cancelling the £30 meal? Remember these verses are an appeal to the 'strong', who are not so disturbed about the issues, with the suggestion there is a deeper consideration than liberty, 'Do not allow what you consider good to be spoken of as evil' (v16).

Believers need to be aware when they have reached a point where an issue threatens to destroy the work of God. At this point, we need to remember that the life of the kingdom is not centred on venues for a church leaders' conference, displays at Christmas or celebratory suppers in a restaurant.

Each of the examples I have provided are a reflection of the pastoral dilemmas I have encountered in my own ministry. In some instances, we changed our plans out of consideration for those who were deeply exercised about a proposal. But this did not always happen. Working on the biblical guidelines for specific conflict issues is a painstaking process. It may involve putting the issues of conflict in writing so everyone is aware of the true nature of what threatens to divide.

When a church I was pastoring faced a major split over issues concerning the style of worship, I wrote an open letter to the membership laying out the reasons for the changes we were considering. We embarked on a long period of consultation, meeting in small coffee groups at different times of the day to suit the various age groups. The leaders met for times of concerted prayer and waiting on God. At the end of the process, there were helpful clarifications to the proposals: the leadership was more aware of the sticking points of disagreement; and for most people, there was a loving agreement to differ. At no time were dissenters excluded.

We can be very correct about 'laws', but the real work of law-keeping is seen in the fruit of righteous, peaceful and joyful lives. Too often the world has seen the evil of our divisions. I recall reading in a national newspaper the story of a divided church where both parties were claiming the ownership of the church buildings. In the end, they went to court over the dispute and the judge ruled that until the court was in a position to adjudicate on the ownership issue, the front door of the church had to be chained and padlocked, and neither party was permitted to use the premises.

This is a sad loss of priorities by those who are called by God to preach that good news which says that because of the person and work of the Lord Jesus Christ, we are loved, accepted and forgiven.

• Seek to relinquish legitimate things for the sake of others (verses 19–23)

As we consider our disagreements, we must ask ourselves the question: is this likely to split the church? Leaders need to be aware of the motives involved. It is sad to have to concede that there are those who thrive on controversy, and their contribution in a debate generates heat rather than light. Whilst there is a proper place for facing conflict and discussing controversial matters, our objective must always be: 'Let us therefore make every effort to do what leads to peace and to mutual edification' (v19). Paul uses a rich and varied word when he says 'edification'. It is used in the Bible for the building of the city of Jerusalem and the establishment of David's kingdom. In this passage, it suggests the combined ministry of God and his people in building up individual believers in their faith.

This work of building up must never be torn down by disputes over secondary issues. We need to address some prior questions when we are in dispute with other believers: how will this action of mine affect the harmony of the church? Should I refrain from exercising my freedom out of consideration for others? Do I have to express my inner liberty in outward fashion on this occasion? Is this conscience issue for me a priority issue for the church?

• Seek to share the burden (Rom. 15:1–3)

Those who are 'strong' are addressed in the opening verses of this chapter. They are asked to keep in mind the central concern, how to endure the irritation of tensions created by Christians with tender consciences: 'We who are strong ought to bear with the failings of the weak and not to please ourselves' (v1). The Greek word for 'bear' is *bastazein*. It has been pointed out that this word appears 27 times in the New Testament, but there is only one occasion when it certainly means 'endure' or 'put up with'. In the vast majority of instances the idea of carrying is definitely present, and it is 'carry' which suits the present context.

This interpretation transforms any disagreement. It suggests that the strong who claim a liberty in the Lord have greater powers of freedom. They are called to help the weaker persons with tender consciences by relieving them of some of the burden they are carrying. J.B. Phillips captures this spirit in his translation: 'We who have strong faith ought to shoulder the burden of the doubts and qualms of others and not just go our own sweet way.' This bearing of the burden is not intended to confirm a friend in his prejudice, but it does imply we are open to please a fellow-believer to 'build him up'. This means we do not give way easily without making them think through carefully their position in the light of God's word.

These are the dispositions we need to cultivate if we are going to handle disagreements creatively in the local church: love and esteem your neighbour from the heart, establish priorities, be prepared to forfeit your own legitimate liberty and go out of your way to share the burden of the 'weaker' person. Paul also suggests that, if we are going to disagree without being disagreeable, we should note the examples we have been given.

• The example of Christ (Rom. 15:3, 7–12)

The second appeal to the 'strong' Christians is they are to tolerate the views of their friends and not use them as an excuse for division. This is what Christ did. If we remember the spirit of Jesus during his earthly ministry, it will be the greatest incentive to us when facing conflict. 'For even Christ did not please himself' (v3), especially when facing insults. He knew that the insults he suffered during his earthly ministry were directed at God. Contempt for Jesus was contempt for the One who appointed him to minister. Knowing that 'the insults of those who insult you have fallen on me' (v3), Jesus willingly stood between the sinner and God. In the Garden of Gethsemane, on trial before Pilate, suffering on the cross, in all these aspects of the Passion, we are to witness how far Christ was prepared to go in enduring hostility and opposition. 'Christ has become a servant' (v8) in order that the long-standing feud between Jew and Gentile might be healed. Paul reminds us that the gulf was bridged between two warring parties because Jesus limited his own freedoms. He submitted to the customs and ceremonies of the Jews. He allowed his body to be mutilated by the rite of circumcision. He who was without sin insisted on a sinner's baptism. The result was that by limiting his own freedom, Jesus was able to reach both Jews and Gentiles; and the two became one.

• The example of Bible characters (verse 4)

The spiritual childishness of fellow-believers can be a severe test. Our patience will be tested to the limits, and we shall need a spirit of endurance to see us through certain conflicts. The apostle says that in the word of

God we shall find this needed encouragement, as we contemplate 'everything that was written in the past . . . to teach us'. We are to be steeped in the resources of the Bible. A study of our relatives in the family of faith is especially beneficial, as we discover how Abraham yielded his rights of seniority to Lot; Moses relinquished his royal privileges in Egypt; Ruth assumed the role of a refugee for the benefit of Naomi and John the Baptist forfeited his own ministry for the sake of Jesus.

Accept one another!

All that has gone before may be summed up in verse 7. Christ did not wait for us to become perfectly good and totally orthodox. He accepted us as guilty sinners, to become saints in the making. Therefore, 'Accept one another, then, just as Christ accepted you, in order to bring praise to God' (v7). The church at Rome was a mixed congregation. We can be certain that the Jewish-Christian party and the Gentile-Christian element were a considerable influence in the church, but the total membership roll in Romans 16 is a cross-section of society, which includes the names of slaves. Other names indicate some members possessed considerable social status. Some commentators have suggested that the wife of the officer who commanded the Roman expedition to Britain is AD43 was a member of one of the congregations in Rome. If this diverse congregation was going to be united in their 'praise to God', and discover the secret of disagreeing without being disagreeable, then they had to accept each other on the basis that Christ accepted them into the same family. This is by grace and without prior conditions.

Meanwhile back at the housegroup . . .

When Rob and Celia finished studying Romans 14–15, they felt they had gained a better understanding of the dynamics of their own housegroup. They had certainly gained deeper insights on how to cope with some of the tensions of their church family.

They thought of the dozens of reasons why their diverse church membership might be expected to quarrel and divide and then remembered the story of the church which was enduring a time of stress. In one of their sharing times, a church member said rather bitterly that their differences had become so great that people were building walls to keep each other out. Then God spoke through another member of the group who suggested: 'Why don't we take the same bricks and build a bridge instead?'

Questions

1. The teaching in Romans 14 and 15 looks at the 'weak' and 'strong' Christians in relation to the choice of the 'right' food to eat. This was a deep concern for the early church but is not really an issue for Christians today. Who do you think are the 'weak' and 'strong' Christians in the circles in which you move, and why?
2. It is fairly common practice among evangelical Christians to judge and condemn individual Christians and churches. Is this to down to ignorance, prejudice or a wrong understanding of the Scriptures? Are there other reasons for such attitudes?
3. Does your church face tensions or conflicts over secondary or primary issues? Can every contentious

issue in church life lead to a restoration of fellowship?

Books

Robert Amess, *Healing the Body of Christ* (Milton Keynes:
Authentic, 2007).
Timothy George and John Woodbridge, *The Mark of
Jesus: Loving in a Way the World Can See* (Chicago
Illinois: Moody Publishers, 2005).
John Stott, *The Living Church: Convictions of a Lifelong
Pastor* (Nottingham: IVP, 2007).

Part five

Bridges to build

Chapter 10

Bridges of reconciliation

Novi Sad is the second largest city of Serbia and a major centre for Serbian culture, hence the nickname of the city: 'Serbian Athens'. Every year, at the beginning of July, during the annual *EXIT* music festival, the city is full of young people from all around Europe. In 2005, 150,000 people visited this festival, which put Novi Sad on the map of summer music festivals in Europe.Ten years ago it was a very different city. NATO was at war with Yugoslavia over the province of Kosovo and Novi Sad was one of the Serbian cities that bore the brunt of the bombing. The bombing left it without all of the three bridges which span the River Danube. Between 1–22 April 1999, the Varidan Bridge, Liberty Bridge and Zezelj Bridge were all totally destroyed and the population of the city was divided down the centre. A few weeks after the bombing had ceased, I travelled to Novi Sad with Hungarian Baptist Aid for a pastoral and humanitarian visit to Yugoslavian Baptists. I heard some heartrending stories of suffering and bereavement. I saw the destruction of buildings and infrastructure, but much more serious were the traumatised lives of men, women and children. One pastor said to me 'Their bodies are ruined and they have become disabled. Their souls are ruined and they have become disturbed. Because the "Christian" West bombed this city, people now refuse to listen to the Good News. We are many times "hauled over the coals" and called enemies, traitors and fifth columnists. It means that our missionary work is handicapped.' The broken bridges of the Danube created a divided city; the destruction of the bridges disrupted the normal life of Novi Sad; the debris of the bombed bridges ruined the economic life of the wider region; neighbouring countries like Hungary and Romania, which used the river Danube to transport goods down to the Black Sea, had been drawn in to the conflict. It took four years of work to remove the debris of bombed bridges which were making the Danube dangerous for river traffic.

Reading my diary from the journey, and looking again at the numerous photographs of this visit, I can't help drawing a parallel with the broken bridges of church life

- Where there is conflict between believers, it nearly always involves the destruction of bridges of fellowship
- Where there have been natural friendship links, such communication is now broken
- The aftermath of conflict leaves behind dangerous debris hidden beneath the waters
- Others not part of the original conflict are inevitably drawn in and their lives suffer
- It takes years for the destructive debris to be removed and the bridges to be rebuilt

If you have read this far, you will have shared my discovery that the call to unity is a strong theme in the New Testament and we neglect the task of maintaining our unity with other believers at our peril. God's work is always hindered by the destruction of the bridges of fellowship. When this happens, it has serious consequences. Turning a blind eye to the resulting destruction surely grieves the Holy Spirit. Those who are spiritually minded and open to the Lord's direction are given the courage and vision to rebuild the broken bridges.

If you do some research on the history of civil engineering, you will discover some interesting features about bridge-building

- Some people are given a vision to build bridges where none have previously existed
- Some bridges are never built because of vested interests
- Some bridges have to be dismantled and rebuilt when their working life is over
- People can lose their lives in the cause of bridge-building

I belong to a large world family of Christians. Our tribe is called the Baptist World Alliance and is a community of over 105 million in 117 countries. Leading Baptist Christians has been likened to the challenging task of 'herding cats'. Like any large family we have our potential for destructive division. I am well aware of the serious divisions that can arise when Christians disagree. These fallouts can last for years and have an impact on succeeding generations. A recent edition of our house magazine, *Baptist World*, focused on the theme of unity and included powerful testimonies of reconciliation, often following years of estrangement.[31]

One of the most moving examples of rebuilding broken bridges is from South Africa. I have walked with my friend Terry Rae for twenty years, and know something of what it has cost him to be a bridge-building peace-maker. Terry has served as General Secretary of the Baptist Union of South Africa. I also honour the leadership of brothers like Paul Mszisa (General Secretary of the Baptist Convention of South Africa) and Angelo Scheepers (General Secretary of the Baptist Union of Southern Africa). I have had a glimpse of the way they faced the broken bridges of fellowship and the courageous spirit with which they worked to rebuild them and maintain the unity of the Spirit in the bonds of peace.

Like many denominations in South Africa, Baptists were historically divided along racial, lingual and doctrinal grounds. The racial divide began in colonial times when Dutch, English and German settlers from Europe came to the southern tip of Africa in search of a better life, and met the African tribes that had previously migrated south.

Racial attitudes and issues played a major role in the broken bridges. These resulted in a major split in the 1980s, when three of the four associations withdrew from the Baptist Union of Southern Africa and formed separate associations. Much suffering resulted because of the division as disputes over property and pensions saw Baptists fighting and turning their backs on each other. The deepest divisions were between the Baptist Union (BU) and the Baptist Convention (BC).

Terry Rae has shared with me many times the story of the key meeting that took place in May 1998 in the town of Colesburg, South Africa. One hundred and eighty people had gathered from the BU and BC, ninety representatives from each group. On the first day of the gathering, they were in small discussion groups in a large hall. The task of each group was to write down on a flip chart the grievances and hurts that had been caused by actions, statements and attitudes of the other group. Some groups kept coming back for more paper. At the end of the first day, each group read out the list of items that represented the pain and hurt of the disunity. These papers were then stuck to the wall of the hall.

They covered one wall from end to end and people were invited to walk silently down this passage of grief. Delegates from both groups, who were entering the process of reconciliation for the first time, wanted to leave the forum and go home. It was the first time some of them had expressed or heard the hurts of their division, and these experiences were still very painful.

After prevailing on everyone to remain and see the process through to the end, no one left. The next day, after a restless night, the devotional time was centred upon the cross of Jesus Christ. For a short while, the gathering looked away from their personal pain and focused upon the sufferings of Christ.

The two groups were seated on two sides of a hall. The neutral facilitator got up and said to the gathering, 'It is now over to you – who will begin the process of repentance and healing?'

Twenty minutes of tense silence followed.

Then one of the BC delegates rose to his feet and looked across at a BU delegate and confessed that he had criticised and spoken evil of his fellow Baptist. He asked for forgiveness. The two men met each other in the aisle and embraced. This started a floodgate of confession and repentance, with scores of people from both sides standing to confess and asking for forgiveness. There was much weeping; there were little prayer groups all over the hall; there were black and white delegates hugging each other and repenting for their behaviour and attitudes of the past.

This went on for five hours without stopping.

Finally, exhausted, they took a brief break. During this time, the communion table was prepared. When they returned to the hall, the two groups sat at the Lord's table together for the first time since 1987. It was an emotional and deeply spiritual event. The General Secretary of the BU served the bread to the delegates from the BC, and then the General Secretary of the BC served the bread to the BU delegates as they remembered the death of Jesus Christ for us. The facilitator then asked them to take two communion cups and go to someone in the hall who had been the object of their pain and bitterness and use the moment to reconcile, sharing the cup together, remembering that Jesus shed his blood for our sins.

At the close of an exhausting day, they all sat in silence for a while. Then one of the BC delegates, a Xhosa woman from the Transkei, got up and went to the wall. She removed one of the pages containing the script of the grievances and came and placed it under the communion table. Then another and another got up and removed the papers from the wall, until they were all placed under the communion table. Another woman got on her hands and knees under the table and packed the papers into a neat pile.

The BU and the BC leaders rose and declared that they would not resurrect the issues that were under the table. They were covered by the blood of Jesus.

To this day, the issues that caused them such pain have not arisen again to damage the continued process of their reconciliation. Other issues have arisen that still need time and concerted commitment to resolve. Both groups have resolved to work towards unity.

In all parts of the evangelical world, we desperately need this form of generous reconciling ministry of rebuilding the broken bridges. I know situations where people have left a local church or Christian organisation

'under a cloud'. The manner of their departure left a lot
to be desired. There are feelings of being treated without
justice. Everything happened with a curt swiftness.
Innocent family members were caught up in the conflict
and some of them have been spiritually damaged. Those
who remain in the local church or the organisation rarely
mention the unresolved conflict from the past. It is like a
locked cupboard which is never opened for spring-
cleaning.

I meet with wounded Christians who cannot serve the
Lord with freedom because a past wrong has not been
dealt with justly. They acknowledge their wrong doing
and have confessed to the Lord their contribution to the
broken bridge of fellowship. But there has been no clo-
sure. I know speakers who have been 'dropped' from
speaking at conferences because doubts have been
expressed about their soundness. Their real concern is
they were never asked to give an account for their
'unsound' views. Everything was based on second-hand
evidence. The pain of the broken bridge is worse than
the burden of never being invited to speak again.

Everyone who moves in the evangelical world has
their store of conflict stories. We all know where the broken bridges are located. The problem is, we look at these
locations as war zones with memorial stones for the
wounded soldiers. We have our version of the conflict.
Who started it? Who fired the first shot? The statistics of
casualties are recalled with great detail. But does anyone
have the vision to mend those broken bridges?

A dominant experience which I encounter every-
where in the world is the capacity of Christians to
exclude one another from full fellowship in the body of
Christ. The pain of exclusion is present whenever ethnic
origins, ancient animosities or doctrinal convictions
become a more powerful force than the bloodline of life

together in Christ in the believing community of the church.

In Latin America, it is sometimes enmity between traditional denominations and newer Pentecostal churches; in parts of Eastern Europe, it can be the superior relationship of the Orthodox church to every other Christian tradition; in the Balkans region, it is the ethnic tensions between Christian groupings; in North America, it is the ideological power of evangelical fundamentalism that excludes others; in Africa, it is tribal loyalties that can murderously divide; and in the United Kingdom, it can be the judgmentalism and lovelessness between evangelicals. What is common to all is the failure to cope with otherness – the simple fact of others being strangely different leads to damaging alienation.

A significant contribution to understanding the pain of exclusion has been made by the Croatian Pentecostal theologian, Miroslav Volf. He lectures at Yale University Divinity School and has written extensively on a theological exploration of identity, otherness and reconciliation, notably in his book *Exclusion and Embrace*.[32] As a Croat, he draws on his personal and painful experience of living with the ethnic hatreds in former Yugoslavia and describes ethnic otherness as a filth that must be washed away from the ethnic body.

Those who encounter the pain of exclusion within the body of Christ need some firm theological foundations in order to survive, and Volf lays these foundations with a wonderful precision. Citing the biblical teaching that those who are in Christ are a new creation (2 Cor. 5:17), he suggests the Holy Spirit unlatches the door of our hearts, saying 'You are not only you; others belong to you too.'

He then provides a wonderful extended word picture which he terms the drama of embrace. Volf describes the four structural elements in the movement of embrace:

the opening of the arms; the waiting for the other; the closing of the arms around the other and the releasing and opening of the arms.

- The *open arms* are a gesture of invitation, saying there is space for another.
- The *waiting arms* are a sign that, although embrace may have a one-sidedness in its origin, it can never reach its goal without reciprocity.
- *Closing the arms* reminds us it takes two pairs of arms for one embrace. Each is holding and being held.
- *Opening the arms* leaves only one outcome. A genuine embrace cannot leave either party completely unchanged. This is why Volf calls this 'the risk of embrace . . . I open my arms and make a movement toward the other and do not know whether I will be misunderstood, despised, even violated or whether my action will be appreciated, supported and reciprocated.'

The more I reflect on this powerful symbol of a physical embrace, the greater potential I see for reconciled fellowship.

I found that sharing the story of truth and reconciliation from South Africa was immensely powerful and a personal challenge as to how we might attempt to mend the broken bridges in our country. How can we take the risk of embrace and build some bridges of fellowship?

As I was completing this chapter, I received an email from a friend who is recovering from what he calls 'abusive behaviour by a Christian leader'. He tells a story of a pastor whose oppressive behaviour goes unchallenged by those still in his church, where he tells those who want to leave that they will forfeit their chance of Heaven and bring themselves and their families under the power of Satan. The hardest thing to cope with, my friend says, is trying to have ongoing relationships with those still in the church, when they do not want to hear and will not listen or react to the testimonies of those their pastor has damaged.

How, in these circumstances, he asked me, do you keep the bond of unity, in the face of such spiritual abuse? Where are the boundaries? When are we free to say, I have tried, but I can't get anywhere? What are our responsibilities to the abuser and the abused? By trying to keep the lines of communication open with the abusive leader, are we legitimising his leadership – and his abuse? And are those who stay condoning his abuse, even colluding with it? Are they therefore also responsible? And should that be challenged?

- Reconciliation is costly.
- Reconciliation takes courage.
- Reconciliation always follows the way of the cross.

Questions

1. The story of the broken bridges of Novi Sad carries with it a message of hope in today's broken world. What hopeful signs do you see across Christian communities in the UK that will enable better relationships to emerge among evangelicals?
2. Look at 'the broken bridges of church life' on page 106. Are there connections you can make with the churches you know?
3. To what extent do you think the account of the eventual 'reconciliation' of the BU and BC churches in South Africa is a public model for all evangelical groups to follow?

Books

Mark Dever, *Nine Marks of a Healthy Church* (Wheaton Illinois: Crossway, 2004).

Phil Potter, *The Challenge of Change – A Guide to Shaping Change and Changing the Shape of the Church* (Oxford: Bible Reading Fellowship, 2009).

Graham Tomlin, *The Provocative Church* (London: SPCK, 2002).

Miroslav Volf, *Exclusion and Embrace* (Nashville: Abingdon, 1996).

Chapter 11

Bridges of community

Someone has said that church life is people coming together for worship without knowing each other; living in the same church fellowship without loving each other; and dying as church members without grieving for each other.

It is a dreadful parody of the church and I doubt whether any one would want to belong to a community like this. I have never encountered church life of such a poor quality and would be ashamed to be a pastor of a church that embraced these appalling values. And yet this parody of extreme individualism in church life draws attention to an important truth about the church. I am a believer called to a life together with other believers. However challenging I find my fellow believers, I am bound together with them in community. God intends me to build meaningful relationships in the church to which I belong. When Jesus appointed the twelve disciples, the first thing we read was he chose them to 'be with him . . .' (Mark 3:14). A meaningful relationship with Jesus and other disciples preceded the sending out of the apostles on their preaching missions. Within this close community of Jesus and the disciples, we have the founding principles of what can be termed life together.

Philip Greenslade, in his classic book *Leadership*, says that being *with* Jesus was to be the basis of doing things *for* him

> He gave himself to them and not merely his principles, spending more time with them than anyone else. He laid down his life for them in countless ways in the years leading up to the cross, letting them invade His precious privacy by their eagerness to be with Him, letting them try His patience by their slowness in learning from Him. He allowed them to see Him tired, hungry and home-less, schooling them in rejection and preparing them for the future as the 'offscourings of the earth' (1 Cor. 4:11–13).[33]

The purpose for mending the bridge of community is that it strengthens our life together as God intended; we follow the pattern of Jesus and his relationship with the twelve disciples; it builds strong and healthy communi-ties; it preserves the unity of the church and it protects its holiness.

I want to explore three related aspects of community in this chapter: life together, loving accountability, and godly discipline.

Life together

I have in my library a dog-eared version of Dietrich Bonhoeffer's *Life Together*.[34] My copy is 42 years old and was inscribed in 1967, the year I was ordained. It has been a treasured part of my devotional reading through the years, and I regularly return to its pages for some fresh insight into the meaning of Christian community.

Bonhoeffer's vision, during the years leading up to World War II, was to sustain disciples of Jesus Christ in their faith at a time when the Nazi party was ruling Germany. He knew that it was a good and pleasant thing when those of like mind can live together in unity (Ps. 133:1). There is a joy and strength to be gained through the physical presence of other Christians. Community life with other believers is an 'inexpressible blessing' and a gift of God that we take for granted. If we are going to be a salt and light presence in the world, we need to be formed as disciples of Jesus in the context of a loving community.

Bonhoeffer was not starry-eyed about life together and warned his readers against the self-centredness which poses as caring love but actually drains energy from the life of a community. He has strong words for those who constantly complain and suggests instead they focus on gratitude to God for his gifts. Moses had complainers in the camp (Ex. 15:24); Jesus faced the grumbling of religious leaders (John 6:41) and grumbling was a sin in the early church (Jude 15–17). It is one of the besetting sins of the church today and, if not confronted, can disrupt the life of a community.[35]

Pastor Bonhoeffer lists three kinds of services that we must offer to one another in Christian community.

The first is *listening to others*. If we cannot listen patiently to each other, how can we listen to God? The second is *active helpfulness*. He has the menial task of service in mind, without which a community cannot function. Bonhoeffer says: 'Those who worry about the loss of time entailed by such small external acts of helpfulness are usually taking their own work too seriously.' The third kind of service is *forbearance*, following Paul's advice that we should 'carry each other's burdens, and in this way you will fulfil the law of Christ' (Gal. 6.2). This means the strong help the weak, the healthy care for the sick, the wise share their wisdom with the less knowledgeable, the mature advise those young in the faith, and the whole community resists the spirit of judgmentalism in its dealing with those who have sinned and fallen.

I had only been a Christian for a few months when my youth leaders, Eric and Margaret Christie, introduced me for the first time during a Bible study to the *one another* passages of the Bible. I was intrigued that the phrase occurred so frequently in the New Testament and the impact of listing all the Bible passages and meditating on them leaves you asking the question: how? How can we submit to the Scriptures in this important area of life together without the experience of deep and meaningful fellowship in community?

Pray and meditate over these *one another* verses from the New Testament. Ask yourself how they could become more of a reality in your friendships and in the life of your local church. What would be the outcomes if national evangelical leaders submitted in fellowship to these Scriptures?

- A new command I give you: Love *one another*. As I have loved you, so you must *love one another* (John 13:34).
- By this all men will know that you are my disciples, if you *love one another* (John 13:35).
- Be *devoted to one another* in brotherly love. *Honour one another* above yourselves (Rom. 12:10).
- Live in *harmony with one another*. Do not be proud, but be willing to associate with people of low position. Do not be conceited (Rom. 12:16).

- Let no debt remain outstanding, except the *continuing debt to love one another* (Rom. 13:8).
- Therefore let us *stop passing judgment on one another*. Instead, make up your mind not to put any stumbling block or obstacle in your brother's way (Rom. 14:13).
- *Accept one another*, then, just as Christ accepted you, in order to bring praise to God (Rom. 15:7).
- I myself am convinced, my brothers, that you yourselves are full of goodness, complete in knowledge and *competent to instruct one another* (Rom. 15:14).
- *Greet one another* with a holy kiss. (Rom. 16:16; 1 Cor. 16:20; 2 Cor. 13:12; 1 Pet. 5:14).
- I appeal to you, brothers, in the name of our Lord Jesus Christ, that all of you *agree with one another* so that there may be no divisions among you and that you may be perfectly united in mind and thought (1 Cor. 1:10).
- You, my brothers, were called to be free. But do not use your freedom to indulge the sinful nature; rather, *serve one another in love* (Gal. 5:13).
- Be completely humble and gentle; be patient, *bearing with one another in love* (Eph. 4:2).
- Be kind and *compassionate to one another*, forgiving each other, just as in Christ God forgave you (Eph. 4:32).
- Speak to *one another* with psalms, hymns and spiritual songs. Sing and make music in your heart to the Lord (Eph. 5:19).
- *Submit to one another* out of reverence for Christ (Eph. 5:21).
- Bear with each other and *forgive whatever grievances you may have against one another*. Forgive as the Lord forgave you (Col. 3:13).
- Let the word of Christ dwell in you richly as you *teach and admonish one another* with all wisdom, and as you

sing psalms, hymns and spiritual songs with gratitude in your hearts to God (Col. 3:16).

- Therefore *encourage one another* and build each other up, just as in fact you are doing (1 Thess. 5:11).
- But *encourage one another daily*, as long as it is called Today, so that none of you may be hardened by sin's deceitfulness (Heb. 3:13).
- And let us consider how we may *spur one another* on toward love and good deeds (Heb. 10:24).
- Let us not give up meeting together, as some are in the habit of doing, *but let us encourage one another* – and all the more as you see the Day approaching (Heb. 10:25).
- Brothers, *do not slander one another*. Anyone who speaks against his brother or judges him speaks against the law and judges it. When you judge the law, you are not keeping it, but sitting in judgment on it (James 4:11).
- Now that you have purified yourselves by obeying the truth so that you have sincere love for your brothers, *love one another deeply*, from the heart (1 Pet. 1:22).
- Finally, all of you, *live in harmony with one another*; be sympathetic, love as brothers, be compassionate and humble (1 Pet. 3:8).
- *Offer hospitality to one another* without grumbling (1 Pet. 4:9).
- Young men, in the same way be submissive to those who are older. All of you *clothe yourselves with humility toward one another*, because 'God opposes the proud but gives grace to the humble' (1 Pet. 5:5).
- But if we walk in the light, as he is in the light, we have *fellowship with one another*, and the blood of Jesus, his Son, purifies us from all sin (1 John 1:7).
- This is the message you heard from the beginning: *We should love one another* (1 John 3:11).

- And this is his command: to believe in the name of his Son, Jesus Christ, *and to love one another as he commanded us* (1 John 3:23).
- Dear friends, let us *love one another, for love comes from God*. Everyone who loves has been born of God and knows God (1 John 4:7).
- Dear friends, since God so loved us, *we also ought to love one another* (1 John 4:11).
- No one has ever seen God; *but if we love one another, God lives in us* and his love is made complete in us (1 John 4:12).
- And now, dear lady, I am not writing you a new command but one we have had from the beginning. I ask that *we love one another* (2 John 1:5).

Loving accountability

Once we begin to experience the richness of life together in a Christian community, we are then faced with the challenge of accountability. Many years ago, I learned this simple formula:

Authority minus freedom = authoritarianism
Freedom minus authority = individualism
Community plus accountability = a church fellowship

I am the person I am because of the grace of God at work in my life, and because I have been surrounded by people to whom I have been accountable since my earliest days as a believer. One of the major causes of disunity and sadness in the church is the lack of accountability in the life of Christians, especially leaders. There are pastors who deliberately choose to lead the life of loners. Never is the saying truer than of the lonely pastor – 'the higher you rise up the ladder of leadership, the less feedback you receive.'

I have had the sad responsibility of being involved on numerous occasions in the discipline of a Christian leader who has abused their position of authority and claimed absolute rights of leadership in pastoring and decision making. They were deluded into imagining their privileged pastoral position meant they were only accountable to God for their actions.

I have often had to confront a church leader on the grounds of 'conduct unbecoming'. The revelation of misconduct has come as a shocking discovery to their family and those nearest to them in leadership. Nearly always, you discover there has been an absence of mirrors in the leader's life. No one has been near enough to reflect back to them their besetting sins and dangerous weaknesses. They had a secret life. Their family and friends were blind, or chose not to see the way they were being ensnared by sin. There was a glaring absence of open accountability. This attitude is a recipe for dividing a church.

This attitude of refusing to be accountable often comes hand in hand with the belief of abusive leaders that they are special, singled out by God and the rules don't apply to them. I heard of one abusive leader who had been having an affair and said he thought God had provided the woman in question as a comfort to him. Leaders with no accountability in their lives often believe their church is the only one that God is interested in, and they have little to do with other churches. They cut their church off from others, they don't go to meetings with other church leaders, and they don't encourage para-church events nor advertise them to their congregations. This lack of accountability in the life of any leader is immensely damaging to their church and brings the gospel into disrepute.

I thank God for my life partner and best friend – my beloved wife Janet. In 1966 we made a solemn marriage covenant and Janet is the first human being to whom I am accountable. I pay tribute to all the leadership groups with whom I have worked. Three churches and one Christian organisation have held me accountable over 42 years of ministry. I know I have been a challenging colleague at times. As one of my close friends says to me, 'David, your ideas have such energy and enthusiasm, we feel we are trying to hold back a carriage hauled by four horses!'

Accountability can be painful. When I am told my big dream is not such a great idea, I am crestfallen. When I am informed that it is a good project but the timing is wrong, I am disappointed. When I am confronted with the bad news that the 'ship' is heading for the rocks and my navigation has steered us towards danger, I am grateful (eventually) for the wounds of truth from a faithful friend (Prov. 27:6).

Nearly twenty years ago, I became a member of a personal accountability group with three other Christian leaders. The membership has changed from the original group but the values of humour and friendship, vulnerability and accountability, prayer and the integrity of confidentiality are exactly the same as at the beginning. We meet four to five times a year, and one of these occasions is an extended prayer retreat. On another occasion we are joined by our wives for a Christmas dinner.

All of us are ordained pastors but not from the same denominational tribe! The essence of the group is to enjoy each other's company so this might include an evening meal and a movie. We might spend the whole of our time focused on the present needs of one member of the group. We always enjoy an honest exchange on the issues of the day – political, cultural and theological. It is not the only friendship circle we move in and, most of the year, we live our lives separately and have accountability relationships with our marriage partners and those we work with day to day. But this 'gang of four' is very special to me.

Central to the life of the group is the time we spend focusing on the personal life and public ministry of each member of the group. The abiding value of the 'gang of four' is that when I am present with the group, I can be myself. Unlike other areas where I minister, I carry no titles. There is no rank or distinction. Nobody line-manages anybody else. There is no 'senior' pastor position. We are just four brothers in Christ and no subject is off limits. I might be challenged over my overcrowded diary; my lack of courage in taking a stand on a public issue; my jaundiced view of another Christian leader or my relationships with my wife, children and grandchildren.

Equally, I might receive wisdom on financial management, encouragement on health matters, advice on organisation strategy or clarification on a point of doctrine. There is always prayer and intercession with passages of Scripture and occasional words of knowledge. Writing this description of the group brings a surge of gratitude to my heart and I publicly pay tribute to Lyndon, R.T., David, Doug, Jeff and John for enriching my life beyond measure.

As I reflect on the years of accountable and vulnerable fellowship with my 'gang of four', I am reminded of the movement founded by John Wesley. When he established the society system in the early days of the Methodist movement, those applying for membership were required to read a list of questions concerning accountability:

- Do you desire to be told of your faults?
- Do you desire we should tell you whatsoever we think, whatsoever we fear, whatsoever we hear, concerning you?
- Do you desire in doing this we should come as close as possible, that we should cut to the quick and search your heart to the bottom?
- Is it your desire and design to be, on this and all other occasions, entirely open, so as to speak everything that is in your heart without exception, without disguise and without reserve?[36]

Godly discipline

Living in accountability with others keeps the personal and corporate body sound and healthy. But there are occasions when normal health and safety provisions have been ignored and direct action is required to preserve the unity of the body of Christ. This calls for truthful confrontation and godly discipline.

When Ananias and Sapphira lied to the church, they had to be confronted with the truth of their dishonesty and the judgment of God was severe (Acts 5:1–11). The story seems harsh to our ears, and some try to rationalise the account by saying the shock of being exposed before the whole church brought on a double heart attack in husband and wife. Even if the terrible discovery killed the couple, Luke is plain that the church understood this as divine judgment for their dishonesty. Whatever the consequences, the passage teaches us the seriousness of church discipline.

When Paul observed that his friend Peter was in grave danger of dividing the church over his behaviour, he confronted him privately (Gal. 2:11) and disciplined him publicly (Gal. 2:14). Whom you choose to eat a meal with seems a minor matter to us, but for the early church, table hospitality was a serious issue concerning the unity of the church.

Peter was the star preacher from the Day of Pentecost, whose exposition of Scripture led to three thousand turning to Christ in one day; the bold disciple who healed a lame man in the name of Jesus Christ; the courageous advocate who fearlessly told the civic authorities that no human law would prevent him from being a preacher of the gospel (Acts 2:14–41; Acts 3:1–10; Acts 4:18–20). This same Peter had reverted to type when he came under pressure from strict conservative believers. Having enjoyed table fellowship with both Jewish Christians who had been circumcised and Gentile believers who had been added to God's family without the need for circumcision (Gal. 2:12), he buckled under the power of a pressure group and began eating at a segregated table for circumcised believers only. By his actions, even good men like Barnabas were led astray (Gal. 2:13).

Paul knew what was in danger from this public behaviour by senior leaders in the church. Two meal tables would lead to two churches; two churches would mean two celebrations of the Lord's Supper; two movements would mean two missions. Peter's behaviour was serious, and it required some truthful confrontation and godly discipline. God gave Paul the insight to come to the heart of what was at fault. Peter was a hypocrite. The Greek word for hypocrite comes from the world of the theatre where it refers to the wearing of a mask or playing a part in a drama. Peter had clearly had the revelation from God that Gentiles like Cornelius were being added to the family of God (Acts 10 and 11). He had defended this belief before the Council of Jerusalem (Acts 15). But in spite of believing something in his heart, he had put on the mask of pretence when it came to table hospitality. Paul rightly called him a hypocrite and challenged him about his inconsistent behaviour.

This does not mean we simply take such passages of Scripture on confrontation and discipline and insensitively apply them to the pastoral situations we face. There can be some major misunderstandings about the nature of church discipline and it is unsound and unhealthy when church discipline is exercised for any of the following reasons:

• *The punishment of offenders?*

The first motive for church discipline is the holiness of God. As David Wells notes, 'It is His being in perfect purity that drives us in the pursuit of what is right . . . it is the people of God showing the same moral seriousness that is in plain sight on the cross.'[37]

At the heart of discipline should be the restoration of a penitent offender and their reconciliation with the rest of the church. To make a public example of someone is the wrong motive from the outset: to imagine that the people being disciplined must be made to suffer in order to compensate for the wrong they have done is to overlook the achievement of the cross of Christ.

God's honour is not satisfied when a Christian is publicly humiliated. Our task is to bring people into a 'walking in the light' relationship with the Son of God who died to deliver us from the kingdom of darkness into the fellowship of light.

• *To uphold standards?*

When a member of a church sins and their moral failure is public, there are those who argue that standards must be upheld. The church must be seen to be taking right-eousness seriously. I share their concern for the moral purity of the church fellowship. But nothing can divide a church as swiftly as the way a church leadership responds to a moral dilemma that arises in the church family. Do nothing and there will definitely be negative reactions. Act hastily without love and justice and another kind of negative response arises in the congregation.

We do not discipline to uphold standards. When we use this legal language, those who have failed have ceased to matter to us. We are more concerned for the standards of the community than the potential reformation of the sinner's life. As we know from his teaching recorded in John 8, Jesus was concerned for both issues and gave priority to the care for the sinner, with the strict command 'go and sin no more'. It is a different matter if someone is bold and unrepentant concerning their sinfulness, and the Bible is clear about this (1 Cor. 5:1–13).

• *To categorise sins?*

The third defective motive for practising church discipline is to categorise sins. We may unthinkingly adopt the attitude that some sins are more serious than others. It goes without saying that sins of sexual immorality, criminal activity and financial dishonesty can be immensely damaging to the church – both within the church family and in the wider community beyond. But the Bible is equal in its condemnation of the sins of pride, greed, slander, lying and an unforgiving heart. If we are going to restore discipline to the agenda, then let us educate a new generation of disciples to expect the widest application of the principles, and let us assure them that leaders will not be excluded from the process.

I recall two members of a church I was pastoring coming to me in confidence and sharing a very serious allegation against one of my fellow leaders. I had to listen to the full details of the accusation which, frankly, I found unbelievable. I knew my colleague as a close friend and could not believe he was guilty of the accusations. But following the meeting with the two members, I went with another elder to see the accused leader. I confronted him with the allegations saying, 'I don't believe this accusation, but I need you to confirm it is untrue.' He calmly denied the charge and assured me the accusation was false.

Armed with this assurance, I went back to the two members and asked them for the source of their information. After a brief reluctance to disclose their source, they relented and, to my shock, named another senior leader in the fellowship as the original source of information. When I confronted him with what had happened, he at first denied being the source, then broke down in uncontrollable weeping, admitting that he had lied.

He went immediately to the accused elder and confessed his sin of lying. He had no grounds for making the accusation. He asked for forgiveness, which was freely granted. All concerned (the wider church family was not aware of what had happened) felt chastened through the experience, and we were more alert to the destructive influence of the father of lies, who loves to divide and scatter the flock of God (John 8:44; 1 Pet. 5:8). Trusting relationships had to be rebuilt gradually and the leader who had failed agreed to a stronger mentoring partnership with a more mature leader in the church.

So why do we bother with church discipline?

- The Scriptures take it seriously. The seriously unrepentant are to be shunned (Matt. 18:15–19); those who create dissension are to be avoided (Rom. 16:17; Titus 3:10); the unrepentant immoral person is to be excommunicated (1 Cor. 5:5, 11); those who are capable of being employed but refuse to work for a living are to be admonished (1 Thess. 5:14); the church is to censor those who are false teachers (1 Tim. 1:3; 2 Pet. 1–22).
- When the church practises healthy church discipline, it coincides with periods of spiritual vigour.
- The ascended Lord delegated authority for discipline to the church, in order to protect his people (Matt. 16:19).
- If the issues of discipline were to be seriously considered by those churches who desire to enhance the unity of the church, it would prove more radical than many of the programmes for church renewal which have emerged in recent years. As John Howard Yoder suggests, 'It gives more authority to the church than does Rome, trusts more to the Holy Spirit than does Pentecostalism, has more respect for the individual than humanism, makes moral standards more binding than Puritanism, is more open to the given situation than the new morality.'[38]

Consider the following questions:

- How many of our pastoral problems would see progress if someone had the courage to exercise some loving discipline?
- When did our church fellowship last examine the scriptural teaching on church discipline?

- Do we continue to pray that the 'prodigals' who have gone out from the fellowship will be restored?
- Does the importance of the offender deter us from taking any action?
- Are our motives right when approaching church discipline?
- Could we be subconsciously seeking retribution?
- Have we struck the balance between the peace of the fellowship and the purity of God's church?
- Are we fearful of the stormy repercussions that might follow the exercise of discipline?

Questions

1. There are 33 *'one another'* verses on pages 119–122. Choose six verses which you think will have the greatest impact on your church life and say why they are so important.
2. What do you think of John Wesley's list of questions on page 126? Are they suitable for today? Would you be willing to be part of an accountability group?
3. Every church has pastoral problems. In your opinion, would we see progress in our pastoral difficulties if we had the courage to exercise loving discipline?

Books

Dietrich Bonhoeffer, *Life Together* (London: SCM Press, 1954).[39]

Geoffrey B. Kelly and F. Burton Nelson (eds.), *The Cost of Moral Leadership: The Spirituality of Dietrich Bonhoeffer,* (Grand Rapids Michigan: William B. Eerdmans, 2003).

Philip Greenslade, *Leadership* (Farnham: CWR, 2002).
James Lawrence, *Growing Leaders* (Oxford: BRF, 2004).
David F. Wells, *The Courage to be Protestant* (Nottingham: IVP, 2008).

Chapter 12

Bridges of witness

I have seen the best and the worst times when it comes to evangelical co-operative mission, evangelism and prophetic witness. I have been privileged to serve for 42 years in Christian ministry in the United Kingdom, over half of these years as a local pastor and the rest as a national leader with special responsibilities for renewing churches with a missionary passion for the spiritual state of our nation. I have visited over seventy countries and seen stunning examples of fruitful salt and light ministries. Many of these ministries are carried out under the hostile stare of atheistic political and government systems, where it is forbidden to change your birth religion. Many people have built the strongest bridges of witness against some unbelievable odds.

The 'best of times' involving united witness have served to enrich my life and ministry. I can think back to days when, under the gifted leadership of evangelists like the late Donald English, there would be town-wide evangelistic missions. I know something of the personal impact that the Making Waves mission had in Plymouth in the 1990s. In the 1980s, I was privileged to be part of Mission Torbay which united churches together in intensive evangelism in churches, schools and workplaces. Through the evangelistic ministry of gifted people such as Eric Delve, Ian Coffey, Max Sinclair and many others, dozens of people who came to faith in Christ are now serving the Lord in church leadership. United in the truth of the gospel and mission outreach, churches were strengthened in their life together.

I have the happiest memories of working alongside Christians of all denominations in 'bringing Christ to the nations'. My mind has been stretched by the enthusiastic visions of a younger generation of evangelical Christians who achieve unthinkable things in the cause of evangelism. I have fond memories of working with my much loved friend Rob Frost, not only through his personal vision of Easter People, but the endless evangelistic enterprises which captured the enthusiasm of local churches. I can recall sharing with Churches Together in Winchester on the eve of their Easter project Winchester Passion. This inspiring project was supported by the greatest breadth of denominations, and with such a passionate prayer concern for the unsaved of their city.

The work of organisations such as CARE is a stunning example of pan-evangelical cooperation and their strap line says it all: 'Making a Christian difference for the sake of the future.' CARE has demonstrated consistently prophetic courage in communicating biblical values in a compassionate way.

I praise God for those churches that get stuck into projects such as 'Soul in the City', Hope08 and the ministry of the Street Pastors project. In all this, I would dare to claim we were fulfilling the prayer of Jesus for his disciples: 'May they be brought to complete unity to let the world know that you have sent me' (John 17:23).

And the worst of times? I can recall a London meeting convened by Joel Edwards, then the General Director of the Evangelical Alliance. He had a vision for a united national evangelistic initiative which would draw on the experience and insights of a host of gifted people who had a heart to see people won to Christ. There were representatives of between fifteen and twenty Christian organisations gathered around the table as we listened, prayed and discussed. At the end of the day, we broke up with no agreement reached and no plans we could pursue together.

What was the reason for this failure? It is possible that the details of the project were not sufficiently honed; it may be there were issues of finance; perhaps the timing could have been more flexible; some wanted a greater leeway in the manner the project would be rolled out; there were the usual suspicions which are present whenever two or three are gathered to discuss a united project: 'The matter has already been decided, and all you are looking for is the rubber stamp of approval.'

I share this story with a heaviness of heart, and take my share of the blame that nothing transpired as a result of the meeting. Others present will have their own interpretation of events, but I think at the root of everything was an unwillingness to sacrifice our organisational identity. We were unwilling to give up our personal plans for anything between one and two years, as this might leave a lasting impact on our identity. Additionally, our prayer support and our organisations might suffer financially as giving was diverted.

I can recall another 'worst time' of broken bridges from the city of Quito in Ecuador. During a visit to the city in 2006, I was invited to a breakfast with representatives of the ecumenical council as well as leaders from some of the leading evangelical para-church agencies working in Ecuador. All the leaders expressed a common concern about the phenomenal growth of the independent mega-churches which are mushrooming in many parts of Latin America. There was an agreement that the old traditional denominations were dying on their feet, and they needed some of the vibrant life present in these newer churches. The sadness for those present was that two or three of the pastors of the largest churches were absent from the breakfast table.

'The problem with the new church', observed a veteran leader of many years, 'is they have no theology of the ancient tree trunk. They think Jesus was born in their back yard and the Kingdom of God began with them. They have no idea that they are a branch in a tree which has a very ancient trunk two thousand years old. This trunk represents the wisdom and experience of God's church through the years.'

This amnesia regarding the ancient trunk is a very secular attitude which infiltrates the church. Tom Oden is a Methodist theologian who emphasises the importance of drawing inspiration from the life of the church in the early centuries of Christianity. He is accurate when he says modern society is xenophobic towards the past. It adores today, it worships tomorrow and it loathes antiquity. All Christians are prone to this attitude and we need to guard against this blinkered approach to church history and present day fellowship. We often make very narrow choices when it comes to friendship and partnership in the family of God, and we impoverish our own mission by such decisions.

Joel Carpenter is an American academic who has conducted considerable research on how evangelicals relate to other churches. He challenges evangelical Christians over their isolation and estrangement from other Christians, and suggests we should ponder what God has been doing in communions alien to our own: 'There is a wideness in God's mercy that we are not fully appreciating and a fellowship we are not appreciating and founts of wisdom from which we are not drinking. Some humility, curiosity and yearning to learn from and have fellowship with other Christians would help us greatly.'[40]

If you find this analysis too pessimistic, then hear me out. There is so much to encourage in current evangelistic enterprise. The most successful evangelistic method of the last twenty years has been the Alpha programme which emanated from Holy Trinity, Brompton. Another evangelical church, All Souls, Langham Place, gave birth to Christianity Explored, which has also been widely used by churches of all denominations. There are numerous evangelistic organisations committed to working in schools and communities. I applaud the fruitfulness of those I have worked with including Saltmine, Viz-a-Viz and Youth for Christ. Sustained and imaginative evangelism has always been one of the strengths of evangelicals, especially through local churches coming together for town and citywide initiatives.

Nevertheless, I contend that the greater our fragmentation, the weaker the impulse for such initiatives. This is the time for evangelicals to share their vision for mission, pool their gifts and talents and offer their resources and experience to the whole church, which so often feels ill at ease with the rapidly changing culture. A local church can see the needs of a spiritually thirsty world, but often feels helpless in directing people to where they can find the wells of living water.

I discern that there are many things to encourage, and good mission practice is in place in many local churches. But I believe mission is frequently more of a headache than a heartbeat for them. Overall, the church in the UK is in deep trouble with persistent decline, serious denominational disintegration and social marginalisation, and statistically there are warning signs that we need to note. I read recently the speech that Winston Churchill made to the House of Commons in September 1941: 'I have heard it said that leaders should keep their ears to the ground. All I can say is that the British nation will find it very hard to look up to the leaders who are detected in that somewhat ungainly posture.'

I agree there is nothing more dangerous than to live in the shadow of a Gallup Poll – always feeling one's pulse and taking one's temperature. But whatever Churchill had in mind, we do need occasionally to take our spiritual pulse and temperature, and that includes reviewing church statistics. I suspect that the published results of any church census will reveal a steady decline in membership for the majority of churches. In 1979, 12% of the population went to church. This declined to 10% in 1989 and 7.5% in 1998. This decreased to 6.3% in 2005, which is 3.7 million people. The projected figure for 2015 will likely bring that number down to 2.4 million of the population as regular churchgoers.[41]

It would be worth examining whether the programmes of Willow Creek, Purpose Driven church and Alpha have been sufficient to offset sharp decline in some churches, or whether all our churches, including those which have followed these programmes, are facing fundamental questions about mission practice. I suspect that the benefits of spiritual renewal, which manifestly have emerged from these valued programmes, have not always spawned the necessary breakthrough into creative mission and evangelism which brings the local church in touch with a growing number of unreached people groups.

Our problem is we see so many changes in the world that we become overwhelmed by the strangeness of the cultures growing up around us, and lack the faith to believe that God is present in them. When the world around us is changing, this constitutes a new calling from the missionary God, because his loving heart for our needy world never changes. God always raises up mission leaders to reconstitute the church as a bridge-building people. These are some of the distinguishing marks of mission leaders.

1. Mission leaders convince the church to ask the right question. It is not 'Where does God fit into the story of our lives?' The real question is where our little lives fit into the great story of God's mission.[42] We are a sent people. Central to everything is the missionary nature of the church that is expressed by its witness to the gospel. Missionary leadership convinces the church it is a sent people, following Jesus in his mission in the world.

2. Mission leaders refuse to domesticate the gospel. They know their task is to challenge churches to engage prophetically with the community where they are placed. They know that worship can become disengaged from mission responsibility and discipleship training can become detached from the duty of witness in the life of the wider world.

3. They discourage church members from being held captive to the culture and needs of the church organisation. They are committed to training disciples to be subversive spiritually for Jesus, in the world of the workplace and the home.

4. Mission leaders encourage the church to know the power of prayer. They constantly direct the local church to the wellsprings of spiritual refreshment and renewal. They are always asking: is this community listening to God? Are the people of God discovering what the Spirit is saying to the church? They promote the principles of healthy church.

5. Mission leaders warn the churches they must be prepared to pay the price of mission. They know that mission ministry is costly and heroic.
6. Mission leaders engage in a preaching ministry that is characterised by its prophetic edge. We need preaching in our time that, in Brueggemann's words, is 'demanding, daring and dangerous'. We need prophetic preachers who can 'use language that shatters fixed conclusions and breaks open old worlds'.[43]

In summary, this is my perspective for bridge-building churches

- They are prepared to offer themselves in prayer to God's mission and his loving purposes in the world
- They understand the importance Jesus assigned to unity and truth in mission
- They are open to experiments in thoughtful evangelism under his leadership
- They are committed to caring and nurturing disciples more creatively
- They are open for engagement with the common questions of our cultures
- They intentionally foster leadership teams with a heart for mission

Questions

1. What, in your view, are the barriers that prevent evangelical Christians working together in mission? What can be done to overcome the reluctance of evangelicals to work together in order to be partners in the Great Commission of Jesus?

2. In the last decade, more creative ways of being church have developed among a younger generation of evangelical Christians. What is your view of these 'new' churches, and is this the answer to our falling church attendance and membership?

3. Six marks of mission leadership have been listed for bridge-building churches. Can you add any further marks to this list or are you satisfied with it? How do these marks relate to your own church?

Books

Tim Chester and Steve Timmis, *Total Church: A Radical Reshaping Around Gospel and Community* (Nottingham: IVP, 2007).

Ian Coffey, *Working it out: God, You and the Work you do* (Nottingham: IVP, 2008).

John Drane, *After McDonaldization* (London: Darton, Longman & Todd, 2008).

Christopher J.H. Wright, *The Mission of God* (Nottingham: IVP, 2006).

Tom Wright, *Surprised by Hope* (London: SPCK, 2007).

Epilogue

The world at one

If the theme of this book is taken seriously, it will give birth to dissent. There are areas of church life where our blind and loveless disunity brings dishonour and disgrace to the name of Jesus Christ. Those who want to dissent from this way of being the church will seek courageously to change the way we relate to each other. But I am aware that people are not changed by exhortation alone. There has to be a new way of seeing things, and our imaginations need to be transformed. We need a fresh vision for our unity which 'purges and refurbishes the Christian imagination'.[44] Reading from the book of Revelation, I believe, provides our minds with such purging and refurbishing.

In Revelation 21:1–8, John presents a vivid picture of the culmination of the gospel story. The entire history of the human race has been moving towards its final destiny. John writes of a new beginning for the whole of creation, and central to this vision is Christ and his church. This new beginning takes place on the very earth where God's purposes have been challenged by sinful humanity throughout history.

- On this earth, where the witnesses have been destitute, persecuted and mistreated
- On this earth, where the Son of God was despised and rejected
- On this earth, where his cross was raised to the sky
- On this earth, where his church has failed in every century
- On this earth, God plans a new beginning

John sees a holy city, the New Jerusalem, coming down out of heaven prepared as a bride beautifully dressed for her husband (Rev. 21:2). 'The bride' is a long-standing Old Testament metaphor for God's people Israel, to whom he is wed in covenant, and 'whose exclusive love and devotion he jealously treasures'.[45]

Jerusalem is the city renowned for its rich worship and its great moments in the history of redemption. This is the city where the tribes went up to worship, singing their songs of ascent concerning Zion, the beautiful city of God. In the city of Jerusalem, prophets, priests and kings foreshadowed *the* One who was to come. In Jerusalem, the early church 'devoted themselves to the apostles' teaching and to the fellowship, to the breaking of bread and to prayer' (Acts 2:42).

But this same city also mocked prophets like Jeremiah, and turned a deaf ear to preachers like Isaiah. This is the city Jesus wept over because the people did not realise the true poverty of their position. The stories of our ancestors in the faith include accounts of great faith as well as extreme frailty. There are inspiring narratives of those who can be commended for their daring faith in God, but there are also stories of broken promises, faithlessness and cowardice.

But through all these biblical stories, God saved people and situations again and again, and this is what makes the story of salvation one of such amazing grace. John is given a vision of the world at one, and which at last includes the people of God in perfect unity. All the tribes – and not just the evangelicals – who confess the Lordship of Jesus Christ are bowed in unity in the worship of the living God (Rev. 7:9–10).

This is the ultimate vision of the world at one that should shape our life together in the Christian community. In this New Jerusalem, some things will be 'no more' (21:4):

- There will be no more sin because the bright light of God's majesty fills the streets (22:5). This is a *holy city* with moral purity.
- There will be no more evangelical culture wars and tribal tensions. Father Abraham was promised descendants as innumerable as the stars in the sky and sand on the seashore, and he was told that all nations would be blessed through him (Gen. 12:3). Well, here they are!
- This is a *cosmopolitan city* with people from all tribes, cultures and nations walking the streets and living in perfect harmony (Rev. 7:9).
- There will be no more excommunications, unresolved issues or unreconciled relationships.
- This is a *peaceful city* where there is no death, pain or tears (21:4).
- There will be no more stains of division; no lines of disappointments; no wrinkles of disagreements. This is the place where the church – God's bride – is dressed perfectly to greet her loved one. This is a *beautiful city* where there is perfect union (Rev. 21:2).
- There will be no more worship wars; no wearisome quarrels over versions of the Bible and patterns of worship; no more endless discussions on the design of

church buildings and worrying debates on expenditure. The shape of this city means it is a perfect cube. In other words, there is no need for a temple, because the presence of the holy God fills the whole city (Rev. 21:3). The ultimate joy of being in the city is at last seeing the face of the Lamb, and his followers are united in their identity, with his name on their foreheads (Rev. 22:4). This is a *worshipping city* with never-ending invitations to the spiritually thirsty (Rev. 22:17).

- There will be no more doctrinal disputes; no more judgmentalism and exclusiveness; no more stories of moral failure and leadership falling by the wayside. The gates of this city are inscribed with the names of the twelve tribes of Israel and the foundation stones of the city are inscribed with the names of the twelve apostles (Rev. 21:12–14). This means the flawed tribes make it there. The frail disciples make it there as well. And by God's grace we too shall be present.
- The flawed, the frail and the faint-hearted are built by grace into the foundations of this city. For this is a *unified city*. This holy, cosmopolitan, peaceful, beautiful, worshipping and finally unified city is our ultimate home.

Until that glorious day, 'The grace of the Lord Jesus be with God's people. Amen' (Rev. 22:21).

Acknowledgements

I am grateful to my late parents Arthur and Elsie Coffey who nurtured my brother and me with a generous and grace-filled expression of the evangelical faith, and taught us to honour all those who named Jesus as Lord, whatever their label.

I thank God for the Keswick movement. It was at Keswick, in the 1950s, that I first heard the call to Christian ministry and, in the 1960s, proposed to my wife, Janet. I remember with gratitude my years of service on the Keswick Council and the stimulating way unity was expressed in diversity. The privilege of being invited to contribute to the Keswick Foundation series on this important theme of evangelical unity carries with it the prayerful hope that the Keswick movement will be an exemplar in fostering the values of spiritual unity contained in this book. I express my warm thanks to my old friend, Steve Brady, who, as series editor, persuaded me of the importance of this theme. Steve did a better job than a church secretary who once phoned me asking me to preach at his church. The secretary said, 'I do hope you are going to say "Yes" as you are the ninth minister I have phoned today!' Steve was gracious enough to leave me with the impression that I was the first person on his list and the best person to write this book.

Soon after I had agreed to the assignment, I was invited by the East Midlands Mainstream Theology group to spend a day with them exploring a weighty theme of my choice. The responses to the paper I gave on principles of evangelical unity laid the foundation for this book, and I am grateful for the stimulating questions and comments from the ministers and leaders attending that day conference. Prior to presenting this paper, I had some fruitful conversations with Marcus Honeysett of 'Living Leadership', and his knowledgeable insights were a shaping influence on some areas of this book.

I enjoy constant conversations with Ian Randall and Nigel Wright of Spurgeon's College, and am grateful for their stimulating friendship and theological insights.

One of the ministers present at the Mainstream Theology Day was Gordon Campbell. We were students at Spurgeon's College in the 1960s, and our families have been friends for over forty years. His enthusiasm for the theme of this book was such that he not only offered to read the manuscript during production but he produced some questions for the end of each chapter. His observations from the world of education and his wide knowledge of the evangelical world have been immensely helpful, and I express to him my appreciation.

The person who carried the greatest faith and patience in believing this manuscript would appear – almost on time – is my editor, Ali Hull. We established the perfect context for my writing temperament which requires a combination of 'stick and carrot' in equal measure. Ali has combined loving encouragement and stern tutelage, and the partnership in writing this book has proved immensely enjoyable.

My final words of thanks go to my family. First, to my brother Ian, whose friendship means more to me with the passing of the years, and his supply of recommended reading and fresh ideas are a constant encouragement. To my best friend – my wife Janet – I express my affectionate appreciation. Regularly she asked me the hard question, 'How is the book progressing?' when she suspected that it was not top of my priorities. She encouraged me like a cheerleader once I commenced the daily marathon of disappearing into the study for hours. Finally, she read the manuscript and offered her own pastoral insights.

I have a number of life verses which summarise my own spiritual values as a disciple of Jesus Christ. Romans 15:7 has always been important to me as a pastor seeking unity for the life of a local fellowship. This verse not only captures the theme of this book, it provides a perfect last word:

> 'Accept one another then just as Christ has
> accepted you
> in order to bring praise to God.'

Endnotes

1   Leon Morris, *Galatians: Paul's Charter of Christian Freedom* (Leicester: IVP, 1996) p123.

2   Health Check article on current state of evangelicalism by John Buckeridge and Ruth Dickinson (*Christianity*, March 2009).

3   Charles Price and Ian Randall, *Transforming Keswick* (Carlisle: Paternoster Publishing, 2000); position statement by the Council in 2000, p268.

4   Rob Warner, *Reinventing English Evangelicalism 1966–2001: a theological and sociological study* (Milton Keynes: Paternoster, 2007).

5   Dave Roberts: 'The debate that won't die' (*Christianity*, May 2008).

6   Terry Virgo, *Blog on Todd Bentley* May 2008.

7   Rob White, article on *The Florida Revival*, www.mainstream-uk.com.

8   R.T. Kendall, web site: article on *Lakeland*, www.rtkendallministries.com.

9   Andy Peck: 'Evangelicals united?' (*Christianity*, January 2008).

10 David Coffey, *Build that Bridge: Conflict and Reconciliation in the Church* (Eastbourne: Kingsway, 1986).

11 David Bebbington, *Evangelicalism in Modern Britain: a history from the 1730s to the 1980s* (London: Unwin Hyman, 1989), p3.

12 Bebbington, p4.

13 See Timothy Larsen in *The Cambridge Companion to Evangelical Theology* edited by Timothy Larsen and Daniel J. Treier (Cambridge: CUP, 2007), p3; and Richard Turnbull, *Anglican and Evangelical?* (London and New York: Continuum, 2007), p58.

14 John Stott, *Evangelical Truth* (Leicester: IVP, 1999), p141.

15 D.A. Carson, *The Gospel According to John* (Leicester: IVP, 1991), p568.

16 Cited by Robert Amess in *Healing the Body of Christ* (Milton Keynes: Authentic, 2006), p57.

17 Derek Tidball, *Who are the Evangelicals?* (London: Marshall Pickering, 1994), p137.

18 A view popularised by evangelical authors such as Greg Boyd, *God of the Possible* (Grand Rapids, Michigan: Baker, 2000) but opposed by John Piper and other evangelicals in *Beyond the Bounds: Open Theism and the Undermining of Biblical Christianity* (Wheaton: Crossway Books, 2003).

19 Centre for Reformed Theology and Apologetics edition of the Westminster Confession Chapter 1 *Of The Holy Scripture* clause 6 see www.reformed.org.

20 R.T. France, *Matthew* (Leicester: IVP, 1985), p317.

21 J.I. Packer, *Fundamentalism and the Word of God* (Grand Rapids: Eerdmans, 1958), pp95-96.

22 Carl F.H. Henry and Kenneth S. Kantzer (eds.), *Evangelical Affirmations* (Grand Rapids Michigan: Academic Books).

23 I am grateful to my friend Ian Randall for this distinction.

24 John Stott, *The Contemporary Christian* (Leicester: IVP, 1992), p193.

25 Carl E. Sanders II, 'The Bible in the American Slavery Debates: Text and Interpretation' in *The Bible in Transmission* (Bible Society, Spring 2007), pp3–7.

[26] John Stott, *The Contemporary Christian*, pp194–206.

[27] From the statement by William M. Kent published in *Report of the Committee to Study Homosexuality to the General Council on Ministries of the United Methodist Church*, August 24, 1991.

[28] R.T. France, *A Slippery Slope* (Cambridge: Grove Books, 2000), p8.

[29] James R. Beck and Craig L. Blomberg, *Two Views on Women in Ministry* (Grand Rapids Illinois: Zondervan, 2001).

[30] Cited by B.N. Kaye and G.J. Wenham, editors of *Law, Morality and the Bible* (Leicester: IVP, 1978), p185.

[31] Terry Rae in *Baptist World* 56:1 January 2009, pp15–16.

[32] Miroslav Volf, *Exclusion and Embrace* (Nashville: Abingdon Press, 1994), pp140–147.

[33] Philip Greenslade, *Leadership* (Farnham: CWR, 2002), pp117ff.

[34] Dietrich Bonhoeffer, *Life Together* (London: SCM Press, 1954).

[35] I have found great help for this section from reading chapter 7 of *The Cost of Moral Leadership: The Spirituality of Dietrich Bonhoeffer*, Geoffrey B. Kelly and F Burton Nelson (eds.) (Grand Rapids Michigan: William B. Eerdmans, 2003).

[36] Cited in Art Gish, *Living in Christian Community* (Scottdale Pennsylvania: Herald Press, 1979), p144.

[37] David F. Wells, *The Courage to be Protestant* (Leicester: IVP, 2008), p241.

[38] John Howard Yoder, 'Binding and Loosing' in *Concern* 14, 1967, p9.

[39] This volume is still in print.

[40] Joel Carpenter, *Pilgrims on the Sawdust Trail*, edited by Timothy George (Grand Rapids Michigan: Baker Academic 2004), p41.

[41] Peter Brierley, *The 4th English Church Census 2005* (London: Christian Research, 2006).

[42] Christopher J.H. Wright, *The Mission of God* (Leicester: IVP, 2006), p534.

[43] Walter Brueggemann, *Finally comes the Poet* (Minneapolis: Augsburg Fortress Press, 1987).

[44] Richard Bauckham, *The Theology of the Book of Revelation* (Cambridge: Cambridge University Press, 1993), p159.

[45] Philip Greenslade, *A Passion for God's Story* (Milton Keynes: Paternoster Press, 2002), p198.